WHO SANK
SURCOUF?

WHO SANK *SURCOUF?*

The Truth About the Disappearance of the Pride of the French Navy

JAMES RUSBRIDGER

CENTURY
LONDON SYDNEY AUCKLAND JOHANNESBURG

Published in 1991 by Century
Random Century Ltd
20 Vauxhall Bridge Road, London SW1V 2SA

Random Century Australia (Pty) Ltd
20 Alfred Street, Milsons Point, Sydney, NSW 2061, Australia

Random Century New Zealand Ltd
18 Poland Road, Glenfield, Auckland 10, New Zealand

Random Century South Africa (Pty) Ltd
PO Box 337, Bergvlei 2012, South Africa

James Rusbridger's right to be identified as the author of this work
has been asserted by him in accordance with the Copyright,
Designs and Patents Act, 1988.

Typeset in Linotronic Times by
SX Composing Ltd, Rayleigh, Essex

Printed and bound in U.K. by
Mackays of Chatham Ltd, plc, Chatham, Kent

A catalogue record for this book is available from the British Library.

ISBN 0-7126-3975-6

CONTENTS

ACKNOWLEDGEMENTS

When I began to research the story of *Surcouf* many naval experts ridiculed my interest and assured me there was no story to tell and that I was wasting my time. But I remembered how other experts had told me the same thing about my researches into similar wartime stories. Most tales about *Surcouf* are easily brushed side as nothing more than rumours and wishful – sometimes evil – thinking. Yet not all can be treated thus. And, in any case, why did this one vessel accumulate such a string of weird stories when other Free French submarines fought so gallantly and were lost with all their crews without any rumours about their loyalties?

Far from there being no story, the history of *Surcouf* has been one of the most intriguing investigations I have ever undertaken. Every time I interviewed someone, or looked in another archive, some new and hitherto unknown fact emerged that threw doubt on previous accounts.

The research for so complex a tale spanned several years and many countries. In Britain, my initial work at the Public Record Office was spearheaded by Dr Muriel Foster who, with her usual tireless efficiency, helped me track down the few scattered files that contained sparse details of *Surcouf*'s unhappy career with the Royal Navy. I am most grateful to Dr Donald Mitchell, Dr Phillip Reed, and Judy Young for their help in locating Roger

Burney's letters in the Pears–Britten archives. Robert Sopwith, the Wellington College archivist, provided much useful material on the time the Burney brothers spent there, and The Revd Professor Henry Chadwick DD FBA, Master of Peterhouse College, was equally helpful with material of Roger Burney's period at Cambridge.

At the Naval Historical Branch I received the usual kind help from David Brown and Lieutenant Commander Michael Wilson RN (Ret'd), but my main source of specialist information came from the Royal Navy's Submarine Museum at Gosport where Commander Richard Compton-Hall OBE RN (Ret'd), its director, and his deputy and archivist, Gus Britton, both distinguished submariners, willingly placed their knowledge and records at my disposal, and were a constant fund of information.

I am especially indebted to the expert advice I received from Lieutenant Commander John Pugh RN, the Wrecks Officer at the Ministry of Defence's Hydrographic Department at Taunton, whose skill at charting *Surcouf*'s last voyage was crucial to the entire investigation, as was the technical help I received from Dennis Pascoe, chairman of Falmouth Ship Repair Yard, Cornwall. Frank Wintle, head of documentaries at Television South West, Plymouth, kindly made available a tape of their award-winning film *Surcouf: Diving to Disaster* which was a most valuable source of background information.

Mrs Joan Adams, sister of Roger Burney, provided an intimate view of their family and Roger's early life and also many letters and photographs. Stanley and Mavis Warner gave me a wealth of information about their uncle, Harold Warner, and made available all his naval documents and photographs. So too did Mrs Lillian Cook, previously Mrs Gough, who, with her daughter Mrs Valerie Buckle, made me most welcome and brought to life the character and career of Bernard Gough. I much enjoyed meeting Fernand Davoult and his wife, who were able to provide such a valuable contemporary account of the problems facing young Frenchmen in Britain in 1940, and his life on board *Surcouf*.

Rear Admiral Sir David Scott KBE CB very kindly made

available his midshipman's diary for July 1940 when he was involved in the takeover of *Surcouf*. My meeting with Lieutenant Commander Francis Boyer RN (Ret'd), *Surcouf*'s second liaison officer, in Dublin provided a unique account of conditions on board, and I am most grateful to him for his willingness to be interviewed at such length.

Mrs Owen Darby, widow of the naval chaplain at HMS *Malabar*, was able to give me a clear insight into the *Surcouf*'s crew while in Bermuda, greatly helped by her friend Marjorie Scadgell who, in 1941, was working as a civilian clerk in the naval dockyard. I am also most appreciative for the help I received from Lawrence Stannard, Colin Davison, editor of *The Western Morning News*, Tom Salmon, and the *Sunday Independent* of Plymouth.

In France, I was assisted by my friend and prestigious historian, Gilbert Bloch, whose expert knowledge of the French archives, coupled with his immaculate instantaneous translations, made my searches and interviews very swift and fruitful. In Paris, the director and staff at the Service Historique de la Marine at Vincennes could not have been more helpful, as were the director and his staff at the Musée de la Marine at the Palais de Chaillot whose collection of photographs and other archival material has added greatly to the book. Mme Thérèse Blaison allowed me to question her for many hours about her husband's naval career and command of *Surcouf*, and very generously made available copies of all his wartime letters to her which make a unique contribution to the book.

In America I was, as usual, indebted to the help I always receive from John Taylor, head of the Military Reference Division at the National Archives in Washington, DC, who with his colleagues Barry L Zerby, Charlotte P Seeley, and William F Sherman provided a mass of documentary material. Their help was matched by James K Owens, director of the National Archives at Waltham, Mass, who provided an unexpected wealth of material relating to *Surcouf*'s refit at the Portsmouth Navy Yard in New Hampshire. The Navy Yard's historian, James Dolph, produced many other new documents together with a wide range of photographs.

My old friend Bernard Cavalcante, head of research at the US Navy Historical Center at the Washington Navy Yard, readily answered all my queries producing a stream of material mainly in the form of ships' logs. I also received much help from George A Walker Jr, head of the US Navy's Oceanographic Office in Mississippi and his colleague, Paul Cooper, at the HYCOOP office in London.

George G Henrikson, special assistant for Security, and John Greenhut PhD, historian of the US Naval Security Group Command HQ in Washington, DC were, as always, most helpful. Commander Eric Berryman USNR of the Naval Sea Systems Command, Washington, DC, was a further valuable source of information. So too was Rear Admiral T A Brooks USN, director of Naval Intelligence at the Navy Department, Washington, DC. I am indebted to Paul Stillwell and Russell A Brown of the United States Naval Institute for publishing details of my research in their *Proceedings* which caught the attention of so many of their readers who contacted me.

Mr Raymond Teichman, the archivist at the Roosevelt Library, once again produced a wide range of documents relating to the political background to the St Pierre and Miquelon affair. David Lawler of the Worcester *Telegram & Gazette* was most generous with his time in helping me trace the widow of Leonard Oates, as was David J Rushford, assistant city clerk at Worcester Town Hall, Mass.

Major Lester A Sliter USAF and Lieutenant David Johnson USAF of the USAF Historical Research Center at the Maxwell Air force Base in Alabama, were instrumental in helping trace the various USAF units stationed in Panama during 1941 and 1942 together with their logbooks for that period. TSgt Barry L Spink, of the Office of Air Force History at Bolling Air Force Base, Washington, DC, kindly provided the entire history of the 3rd Bombardment Squadron during its period at the Rio Hato airbase in Panama, and SSgt Randolph J Saunders, historian of the USAF 6th Strategic Wing at Elsion Air Force Base in Alaska, provided further valuable information. As a result of their help I was able to interview Colonel Harry Staley in Batavia, New York, and Colonel Art Irwin in Navato, California, which provided particularly vital information.

I am especially grateful to the editors of *Air Force Times* and *Aerospace Historian*, who both published stories about my research, which led to many retired USAF personnel contacting me, and the US Air Force Military Personnel Center at Randolph Air Force Base in Texas, who generously used their computer resources enabling me to trace surviving members of units that had served in Panama in 1941–2. As a result Major General William E Creer USAF, Major-General A Yudkin USAF, Major General Robert W Burns, Lawrence Ghiorse, Colonel Howard F Bronson, Colonel Richard W Simons, Jack Schade, Lieutenant Colonel G Robert Fox PhD, and Colonel John P Lippitt all took the trouble to contact me.

Mrs Amy Musher of *Time* magazine very kindly provided archival material from their files about *Surcouf* in 1941. Mrs Henry Smythe in South Carolina (formerly Miss Mary Ridgeway) provided important information about her memories of Roger Burney in Bermuda in 1942, and Mrs Joan McGillary (formerly Miss Joan Mitchell) in Florida gave me many fascinating details of her father's wartime activities.

In Canada I owe a great debt of gratitude to Dr William Douglas, director of history at the National Defence Headquarters in Ottawa, and his researcher Lillian Grantham, who between them turned up a massive collection of valuable material. Also in Ottawa I had the great pleasure of meeting Louis Audette OC QC who, in 1941, was the Royal Canadian Navy's liaison officer to *Surcouf*. I also had the pleasure of interviewing Vice Admiral HG De Wolff CBE DSO DSC CD RCN (Ret'd) who, as Flag Officer to HMCS *Stadacona* in Halifax in 1941–2, was Director of Naval Operations and intimately involved in the movements of *Surcouf* during the St Pierre and Miquelon affair.

In Halifax many people remembered *Surcouf* and her crew, and amongst those that provided much valuable material, including several rare photographs, were Ronald Wallace, the Mayor of Halifax, Ruth Graham, Mrs Earle MacDonald, Roger

Edge, assistant editor of the *Halifax Herald*, and his defence correspondent Jim Gowen, David Perkins, Malcolm Capstick, Frank Tobin, Margaret J Campbell, head of the Photographic Department of the Public Archives of Nova Scotia, Marilyn Gurney, director of the Maritime Command Museum, Graham McBride, curator of the Maritime Museum of the Atlantic, and his charming librarian, Mary Blackford.

In Bermuda, where *Surcouf* is vividly remembered, the arrangements for my visit by Bryan Darby were extremely successful, especially the broadcast and phone-in on VSB Radio, skilfully handled by Shirley Dill, that produced a mass of replies from listeners.

Amongst those that provided essential information were Herbert Tatum, Whitey Froud, Walter Seymour, Donald Bernard, Alexander Frith, William King, Commander Geoffrey Kitson RN (Ret'd), June Stanton (formerly Miss June Ridgeway), René Northover (formerly Miss René Brass), Graham Copeland, Sydney Morgan, Lawrence Dill, and William King. David White, editor of the *Royal Gazette*, kindly produced much useful material from his archives, while the assistant editor, Kevin Stevenson, was able to give me a fascinating account of his many meetings with Sir William Stephenson. Timothy Hodgson, editor of the *Mid-Ocean News*, provided some most interesting correspondence and other background material abut *Surcouf*'s final days in Bermuda.

In Panama, the ground for my visit had been well prepared in advance by John Mann, a Cuna Indian expert for over thirty years. With his help and the incredible skill of my pilot, Krish Persaud, who safely landed me at tiny, remote airstrips in all weathers, I was able to visit San Blas, Panama's Shangri-la, with its kind and gentle Cuna Indians who turned out so willingly to ferry me in their canoes to the various jungle sites. I am also most grateful to Ken Jones and Ted James, editor of *El Boletin*, for all they did to make my visit such a success.

To sustain this quest over so many years I was consistently encouraged and supported by Andrew Lownie who helped turn a string of ideas into a cohesive story, Brian Sweet for his brilliant

ACKNOWLEDGEMENTS

artwork, and my patient publisher, Mark Booth, whose enthusiasm and critical judgement brought the story to fruition, whose skill has turned a fragmented narrative into a book that I hope will be as interesting to read as it was to write, and set to rest the many unpleasant stories that have clouded the memory of this submarine and its brave crew for far too long.

James Rusbridger
Cornwall 1991

CHAPTER 1

THE BLOODY TRICOLOUR

Dawn broke warm and sultry over the naval dockyard at Devonport on July 2 1940. There was a hint of a thunderstorm as clouds began rolling in lazily from Cornwall ahead of a trough of low pressure. *Surcouf* lay in the outer berth alongside the French battleship *Paris*[1] in No. 5 Basin.[2]

She had been moved there three days earlier, the excuse being given that her downstream moorings were needed for other vessels. But the captain, Commandant Martin, and his officers were in no doubt the move was to stop them from making a sudden dash for the sea, and they could hardly fail to notice that the 15-inch guns of HMS *Revenge*[3] just across the basin were trained on them.[4]

Already relations between the French and British were growing increasingly uneasy, and Martin was still very suspicious about the unexpected visit a few days earlier of Vice Admiral Dunbar-Nasmith, C-in-C Devonport, and Lieutenant Patrick Griffiths from the submarine HMS *Rorqual*. Although supposedly a friendly visit, the atmosphere had been very strained and Martin suspected the real purpose had been to enable the British to inspect *Surcouf*'s internal layout should they decide to seize the vessel by force.

What the British did not appear to realize was that the *Surcouf* – like all the other French ships now in Devonport – was

1

still in direct radio contact with Admiral Darlan at naval head-quarters in France. On June 24 Martin had received a coded message from Darlan ordering him to prepare *Surcouf* for scut-tling. The torpedoes were to be defused, the gyroscopes dis-mantled, diving motors and controls were to be wrecked, and all confidential papers burnt. Martin was shocked at these instruc-tions and very reluctant to carry them out because he still believed the British were his allies.

Gradually the great submarine came to life, but there was little sense of urgency amongst the crew as together with what-ever help they could get from the dockyard they continued try-ing to make their unwieldy ship seaworthy again.

The thin, heavily censored newspapers had little good to re-port. With the French armistice now a week old Britain stood alone while just across the Channel, Hitler's victorious armies were regrouping for the seemingly inevitable invasion. Never-theless there was an air of unreality about some of the stories that morning. A Mr Rowe of Vapron Road, Plymouth, wrote warning owners of chickens that they might sometimes appear dead after an air raid but that this was only shock. Advertise-ments for servants still abounded with a 'remote Dartmoor hotel' seeking a couple to run the bar and do the cooking for a live-in wage of three pounds per week. On a less happy note the owner of a 1938 Morris 14-hp car about to join the forces offered his prize possession for a quick sale at eighty pounds.

Tucked away on the front page of *The Western Morning News* was a small bland advertisement from the clearing banks, casually announcing that communications with their Channel Island branches had been temporarily suspended and that, until further notice, letters should be sent to their London offices. In fact the Channel Islands[5] had been occupied by the Germans two days earlier but, in order to sustain morale on the home front, no official announcement had been made about this first loss of British territory to the enemy.

The heat made progress slow and in the *Surcouf*'s engine room temperatures soared as the huge Sulzer diesel engines were tested sending out clouds of black exhaust smoke into the

2

lifeless air. By the end of the working day everyone in *Surcouf* seemed just that little bit more irritable and tired. For the crew it was time to clean up and go ashore for a drink. Hopefully they would have some fun and take their minds off their families and homes in France.

Most of the crew made their way to Union Street where, despite strict wartime restrictions, there was still plenty of night life. Others went to the Palladium cinema to watch Will Fyffe in – ironically, as it transpired – the film *They Came By Night*. And as they watched, drank, danced and flirted Churchill's plan to take over or destroy the French fleet – *Operation Catapult* – got under way.

The long hot evening slowly drew to an end. The blackout began at 10.02 pm and the whole city and dockyard became a ghost town as the bars and cinemas closed and the sailors made their way back to their ships. *Surcouf*, like all the other French vessels in Devonport that night, had been placed on full alert and when all her crew were back on board Martin ordered the hatches closed except for the conning tower. Here a petty officer was stationed while two armed sentries were posted on deck at the head of the gangplank that led from *Surcouf* to the *Paris* alongside.

Gradually peace descended. The ships chafed at their moorings moving uneasily in the swell. The thunderclouds from the west that had kept the air humid throughout the day had at last arrived and a light rain started to fall. Midnight came and went. Watches were changed. Meanwhile there was great activity on board *Revenge*. At 1.30 am, by now July 3, all the midshipmen were called and told to muster outside the commander's cabin. Amongst them was nineteen-year-old David Scott[6] who later wrote in his midshipman's journal:

With mixed feelings we dressed hurriedly most of us
expecting that we had committed some unforgivable
crime, whilst others thought that [German] parashoot
[sic] troops must have landed. All we were told,
however, was that the lower deck was to be cleared . . .

3

and that we were required to call the officers.

Half an hour later *Revenge*'s crew had been mustered and Commander H L Jenkin addressed them:

> The ship will not sail this morning and the reason for this
> early call is that we have been ordered to board the
> French ships in the hope they will agree to remain pro-
> Ally. We have to board the *Paris* and *Surcouf*. It is
> necessary that great politeness should be observed but at
> the same time you must be firm. It is hoped that force
> will not be needed but you must be prepared to meet
> resistance. Avoid provocation and excitement. Silence is
> the watchword until we get on board.[7]

To help the British officers communicate with the French each was given a hastily typed list of expressions which began cordially enough with *'nous sommes la marine Britannique'* ('we are the British navy'), followed by *'nous sommes vos camarades'* ('we are your friends'), and then became rather more officious with *'montez'* ('go up on deck'), and finally *'levez vos mains'* ('raise your hands').

Meanwhile on board *Surcouf* most of the officers turned in, suspecting nothing. At 4.15 am the telephone shattered the silence. The radio operator had just received an 'officer only' coded message from Darlan's headquarters in France and needed the duty officer, Lieutenant Crescent, to come and decode it. Crescent hurried to the radio room, unlocked the safe, took out the codebook and began to turn the message into plain language. He stared in amazement at the text which stated that the Royal Navy were about to attack the French fleet at Mers-el-Kebir and that *Surcouf* was to be scuttled.

Crescent raced back to the wardroom with the message and showed it to Martin but, at the same moment, the petty officer in the conning tower called out that the British were boarding the ship. Crescent ordered 'action stations' to be sounded while Martin gave the prearranged signal that *Surcouf* was to be scut-

4

tled and her vital equipment destroyed. Before any of this could happen, armed British naval officers and Royal Marines dropped down through the conning tower and with guns drawn faced the astonished French crew. In a matter of moments, they had taken control of the submarine.

The French had been caught completely off guard[8]. While they had been watching the gangplank from the *Paris*, a boarding party of five officers and twenty-eight ratings from the submarine HMS *Thames*, led by Commander Dennis 'Lofty' Sprague and Griffiths from *Rorqual*, together with a platoon of Royal Marines from the *Revenge*, had arrived out of the dark in three launches on the other side of *Surcouf* from across the basin. The boarding party had hidden under the seats of the boats so that they appeared empty and only as they drew alongside did the sailors and marines jump up and leap on board the *Surcouf*. Within minutes the submarine was in their hands.

What happened thereafter has been recorded by several people and, as one might suspect in such tragic and traumatic circumstances, their accounts vary considerably.

The British version[9] is that Sprague asked all *Surcouf*'s officers to assemble in the mess room where he read out an order from Admiral Cayol of the flagship *Paris* inviting them to join the Free French navy under the command of Vice Admiral Emile Muselier. The officers were so stunned by what had happened that at first no one spoke. Then Martin told Sprague that he could not believe Cayol had agreed to serve under de Gaulle and said he wanted to hear this personally from Cayol himself. Sprague agreed and Martin left the mess room and was allowed to go over to the *Paris*.

This left Sprague and Griffiths facing the rest of *Surcouf*'s officers in an increasingly hostile atmosphere. Tension rose and clocks seemed to stand still. When, after fifteen minutes, Martin had not returned Griffiths became impatient and ordered all the French officers to leave the vessel. Fearing their captain might have been arrested by the British, the French refused until Martin returned with an answer from Cayol. Stalemate continued with neither side wishing to use force or lose face.

5

Then Lieutenant Pichevin gave a note to one of his ratings who went to the main switchboard and pulled the main switch which plunged the ship in darkness. He was spotted, however, by a petty officer from the submarine *Thames* who hit him over the head with a hammer and immediately turned the lights back on again. The British version claims that one of the officers went to the toilet where guns were hidden but this is at variance with other accounts. Nevertheless Sprague and Griffiths were becoming increasingly uneasy and, when the French refused to leave their ship, firing commenced.

The *Surcouf*'s doctor,[10] Le Nistour, recorded in his statement after his return to Toulon in December 1940 that he was in bed asleep and at 4.30 am was awoken by Crescent shouting, 'The English are coming'. He got up and dressed while Lieutenant Bouillaut opened the revolver rack near his cabin and distributed guns and ammunition to all the officers. When Le Nistour got to the mess room he found all the officers there except Bouillaut and facing them Sprague, Griffiths, a midshipman, and three armed sailors.

Sprague was pale-faced and kept mopping his forehead. His reply to Martin's protest was 'I am sorry. I have my orders.' Le Nistour remarked in his statement, 'How often we would hear that refrain, an excuse for everything in the eyes of the English!' Martin went off to confer with Cayol leaving Pichevin in charge and Sprague became more nervous. Suddenly he ordered all the officers to disembark but Lieutenant Crescent very pluckily retorted that they would only go when Martin returned and ordered them to do so. At this Sprague lost his patience and repeated his order to Crescent in French adding, 'If you don't go, I will kill you'. Crescent replied, 'Carry on and shoot. I'm not moving.'

At this point Le Nistour rushed back to his cabin where he found Lieutenant Daniel, the engine-room officer, busily tearing up plans and secret papers and told him that there was serious trouble in the mess room. Simultaneously shots were heard and what Le Nistour describes as a 'sergeant', but who was actually Leading Seaman Webb, came rushing into the cabin with his rifle and fixed bayonet. Le Nistour immediately opened fire and mortally wounded Webb in the chest, but not before Webb had also mortally wounded Daniel. Another sailor followed Webb into the cabin, and Le Nistour hit him several times with the butt of his revolver, finally knocking him to the floor unconscious.

By the time Le Nistour got back to the mess room the shooting he had heard earlier was over. Bouillaut, who had been slightly wounded in the exchanges, was explaining to Crescent that he had only opened fire in self-defence because he thought the British were going to shoot him. Le Nistour later wrote:

> That's what I think too. Only the speed of Bouillaut's shot saved Crescent from being killed.

But as Le Nistour was not in the mess room at the time it is difficult to see how he could have known what had happened.

By this time the British boarding party had retired to the safety of the central control room (above the mess room) and Pichevin decided there was no point in continuing to resist. Pichevin called to the British that they were surrendering and the crew were ordered to come up singly so that they could be searched.

Le Nistour stayed behind to comfort Daniel who was dying and then went to see what he could do for Sprague (who had been shot by Bouillaut) who was leaning against the bulkhead wounded in the shoulder and abdomen. Le Nistour found one of the shots had entered below the shoulder and severed a main artery. There was nothing he could do to save him. Griffiths lay on the floor beside him also dying. At this point Le Nistour was ordered to join his colleagues in the control room.

The atmosphere there was naturally jumpy with the British covering the French with drawn revolvers. The sailor Le Nistour had clubbed staggered in covered with blood and demanded that Le Nistour be arrested as his assailant, but nothing was done about it. Le Nistour then gave Bouillaut some first aid in the ship's infirmary ignoring requests from the British that he should

7

help their wounded, too.

As Le Nistour and his colleagues were being led off the *Surcouf* across the *Paris* naval medical teams and ambulances arrived. The French were kept at the naval barracks until 11.30 am when they were allowed back on board to collect their private possessions. Le Nistour wrote:

> An English ensign [midshipman] advised me only to take
> what I really needed and gave his word of honour that
> the rest of our belongings would be boxed up and sent
> on to us. One more promise betrayed!

One final upset was caused when the British refused to allow the French to attend the funeral of Daniel and instead bundled them under armed guard into locked carriages on a train bound for Liverpool.

Bouillaut's account, which he wrote on July 25 1940 while in Walton Hospital, Liverpool, is particularly significant because he admits killing Sprague and Griffiths. He, too, had been in bed when Crescent told him, 'The English are here and four are already in the central station [control room]'. Bouillaut had dressed, put his loaded automatic with a spare magazine in his pocket and then unlocked the revolver rack so that each officer could have a gun and ammunition. He then went up to the control room. Here Martin told him to destroy all confidential documents which he went back to his cabin with Daniel and started to do.

After that Bouillaut returned to the mess room where he found Sprague ordering the officers to leave the submarine. When Crescent refused Sprague shouted at him, 'If you don't get going, I'll kill you', to which Crescent replied, 'I'm not moving'. Sprague and Griffiths both took out their revolvers and Griffiths turned to an armed sailor and said in French 'Kill that man', pointing to Crescent. Since it was unlikely the sailor would understand the command in French, presumably Griffiths said it to frighten Crescent but, instead, Bouillaut believed they *were* about to be shot. As he put it in his report:

8

I felt absolutely certain that since Lieutenant Crescent seemed determined to die rather than move, the English ... would have to kill him. I had not received any orders to use my weapon to resist the English but this was not a situation in which one waited for orders.

Without warning Bouillaut stepped forward and opened fire at Sprague, Griffiths and two sailors in the course of which he was also wounded. He then heard the shots coming from below as Le Nistour fired at Webb. When the shooting stopped Crescent said to Bouillaut, 'We've shown our colours but I think you were wrong to do that.' 'But he was going to kill you,' replied Bouillaut. Crescent shrugged, 'So what?'

Although Bouillaut argued they should continue to resist, he was persuaded by Crescent and Pichevin to surrender, and then lay down in the infirmary for half an hour where Le Nistour dressed his wound. When an ambulance arrived, he was taken to nearby Stonehouse naval hospital.

Considering the circumstances it is hardly surprising that claims as to who fired first conflict. Although Bouillaut's account makes it clear that he deliberately fired at Sprague and Griffiths, another British version claims that a nervous British petty officer accidentally discharged his gun. Whatever the truth a blood bath followed. Sprague was hit in the neck and Griffiths in the chest. Webb was killed instantly with a bullet in the chest while his companion, Able Seaman Heath, suffered seven bullet wounds in the face, arms, and neck but happily survived. In the returning fire Daniel was killed by two bullets in the heart while the *Surcouf*'s gunnery officer was badly wounded but survived. All the wounded were rushed to Stonehouse naval hospital but Griffiths and Sprague both died the next day.[11]

After surrendering, *Surcouf*'s crew were taken ashore and marched under escort to the Royal Naval barracks at Hamoaze. No charges were ever made against any of the French over the deaths of Sprague, Griffiths and Webb. Later in the day, small groups were allowed to return and collect their personal belongings, and the atmosphere was further soured when many allegations were made by the French that the British boarding party had looted their possessions. This was strongly denied by the British authorities and the pressures of war precluded any inquiry from being held.

After this *Surcouf*'s crew were put on a special train with armed guards – including some of the Royal Marines who had seized the submarine – and taken to an internment camp at Aintree near Liverpool. By this time news of the Royal Navy's attack on the French fleet at Mers-el-Kebir (see Chapter 3) had become known together with the terrible toll of nearly 1500 casualties. Not surprisingly only sixteen officers and men agreed to return to *Surcouf* and serve in the Free French navy.

Martin was not among them. For him the sight of his proud ship being forcibly taken over by a supposed ally and one of his officers shot dead was too much. For the first time since the Battle of Trafalgar in 1805 French and British sailors had fought each other in hand-to-hand combat. Martin and the rest of his crew were later repatriated to France where their stories of what happened were to poison the future career of *Surcouf* and those Frenchmen who subsequently served in her. The British never fully trusted *Surcouf* again and the French equally never forgave the British. It was hardly surprising that in this bitter atmosphere of distrust rumours grew quickly.

Surcouf herself lay at her her berth empty and abandoned, her decks still wet with blood. No flag flew from her mast. She appeared to have lost her soul and perhaps the will to fight. It was the beginning of the end of her life as a living ship.

NOTES

1. Built in 1912 the 25,850-ton *Paris* was obsolete before the war began and had for some years been used only for training purposes.
2. This part of the dockyard has disappeared with the construction of the Polaris submarine refitting complex.
3. A 29,150-ton battleship built during World War I which by 1939 was too slow and old to be of much value and was mainly engaged on convoy duties.
4. Interview with Mr John Kay, Falmouth, Cornwall, June 1990.
5. Located only forty miles west of Cherbourg and eighty miles from the

nearest English coast, the group of nine islands obviously could not be defended once the Germans had occupied France. Having given members of the population the opportunity to leave for England the British government advised the Germans that the islands would not be defended. Ironically the Germans spent most of the war building enormously complicated defences which had no strategic purpose and were never used. German occupation ended on May 9 1945.

6. Now Rear Admiral Sir David Scott KBE CB.
7. Commander Jenkin's handwritten memorandum kindly made available to the author by Rear Admiral Sir David Scott.
8. Jean-Jacques Antier, *Le sous-marin Surcouf, un tournant de son histoire* (*Neptunia Magazine*, Paris, December 1985), 42–6.
9. ADM 199/822 (PRO, Kew).
10. The reports of both Le Nistour and Bouillaut are in File TTY/683 at the *Service Historique de la Marine* (Vincennes Archives, Paris).
11. Sprague, Griffiths, Webb, and Daniel were buried with full military honours at Weston Mill cemetery on the outskirts of Plymouth. In 1948 Daniel's body together with twenty-six other French servicemen buried there were exhumed and taken back to France. The other three lie at Weston Mill to this day. The *Surcouf* incident was so sensitive and embarrassing that the censors allowed only the barest details to appear in the newspapers for fear of upsetting Anglo–French relations even further and giving the Germans a propaganda coup. Even Churchill was not told of the two officers' deaths and, in 1949, wrote personally to Mrs Sprague apologising that his own book *The Finest Hour* failed to mention their loss. *Submarine Warfare*, Commander Richard Compton-Hall (Blandford Press, 1985).

CHAPTER 2

THE GRAND DESIGN

At the start of World War I submarines were still in their infancy. The Royal Navy's first submarine, HM Submarine Torpedo Boat No. 1, better known as the *Holland 1* after its American inventor John P Holland, was built under licence by Vickers at Barrow-in-Furness and launched on October 2 1901. Four more were built the next year. The *Holland* boat with its seven-man crew, small petrol engine and tiny batteries, was typical of submarines then in service in many countries and of no military value since its range was limited to 200 miles on the surface at 9 knots, or twenty miles underwater at 3 knots, hardly enough to move against a normal tide. It possessed only one torpedo tube and had no periscope. It was not until 1908 with the completion of the first diesel-engined D-class that Britain had its first true fighting submarine.

By August 1914 about one hundred submarines had entered service with the Royal Navy but when set against the battlefleets of mighty *Dreadnoughts* with their massive 12-inch and 15-inch guns the submarine seemed puny and unimportant. Furthermore, many naval officers considered underwater warfare ethically distastefully.

But the submarine service had one formidable supporter. Admiral Sir John Arbuthnot Fisher – 'Jacky' Fisher to his friends and more numerous enemies – the First Sea Lord. Fisher was above all a gunnery expert and enthusiast. He believed in big battleships with big guns. It was entirely due to Fisher that the *Dreadnought* class of battleship was built which revolutionized naval gunnery and tactics not only in the Royal Navy but eventually in every navy around the world.

Fisher also had quite incredible foresight. In 1904 when his battle to build the *Dreadnought* had been won he alone perceived the future menace of the submarine and using his privileged position wrote to King Edward VII warning him of the battleship's greatest potential enemy. No one took any notice.

Germany had also been experimenting with small petrol-driven coastal submarines but the advantages of the diesel engine soon became obvious: it enabled the submarine to make long journeys away from its base, diving when necessary on electric motors, and therefore hidden for as long as its air supply allowed. As a result, by the start of World War I they had a small fleet of *U-boats*, mainly of the 800-ton size, that were soon to prove their worth. Within the first five months of hostilities commencing German *U-boats* had sunk one battleship, five cruisers (three of them – *Aboukir*, *Cressy*, and *Hogue* – by the *U-9* in one morning with the loss of 1459 officers and men), a seaplane carrier, and a submarine. Suddenly Britain's supply lines were so vulnerable to this new undersea menace that at one point in the war the *U-boat* attacks nearly brought Britain to the point of defeat.

In May 1915, at the age of seventy-four, Fisher resigned the post of First Sea Lord. Despite much controversy he was appointed chairman of the Board of Invention and Research (BIR) with offices at Victory House in Cockspur Street. The exigencies of war produce many unexpected talents and ideas since necessity is the mother of invention and the purpose of the BIR was to co-ordinate them and promote the best. One of the earliest was a rudimentary form of ASDIC (Anti-Submarine Investigation Committee), the forerunner of today's sonar for detecting submarines underwater.

On August 5 1915 Fisher proposed to Arthur Balfour, First Lord of the Admiralty (which was a political appointment) that a submarine *Dreadnought* be built fitted with a 12-inch naval gun. The idea was debated over the next six months and it was finally agreed that the submarines *K-18* and *K-19*, then under construction at Vickers, and the *K-20* and *K-21* under construction at Armstrong Whitworth, should form the new *M-Class*.[1]

By the standards of the day these were huge vessels: 300-feet long and displacing over 2000 tons. In addition to the 12-inch naval gun and its mounting which weighed 122 tons, capable of firing an 850-pound shell nearly 19 miles, each submarine was to be equipped with four 18-inch torpedo tubes and a 3-inch gun making them almost nuclear in terms of contemporary fire-power. Each vessel was powered on the surface by twin 2000-hp diesel engines, with a cruising range of 4000 miles at 11 knots, and required a crew of sixty-five officers and ratings, twenty-seven of whom were gunnery experts.

Work continued on *M-1* throughout 1916 but, in 1917, Fisher suddenly got cold feet. He was worried that if the Germans learned of the plan they too might build monitor submarines and bombard Britain's undefended east coast. As a result for a year all work stopped and the four hulls lay deserted. Eventually work restarted and *M-1* was finally launched on July 9 1917 and by March 10 1918 had carried out her first gunnery trials. A month later *M-1* joined the Royal Navy and by June 1918 was fully operational.

M-1's first tour of duty was in the Mediterranean and lasted eighteen months. It had been intended she would shell Turkish positions near Constantinople, but the minefields and uncharted waters of the Bosporous were considered too dangerous. As a result *M-1* saw no action before the war ended in November 1918. *M-2* and *M-3* were not completed until after the armistice and *M-4* was scrapped shortly after her launching in July 1919.

As *M-1*'s fighting potential was never tested in war it is impossible to judge whether she could have been of any tactical value in a naval battle. In theory *M-1* would break surface only long enough to fire her gun and then submerge. This operation took between 40 and 50 seconds. But the gun could not be loaded underwater so the submarine had to surface to do this.

The firing procedure was complicated by the fact that part of the gun turret was wet and part dry, with a complex arrangement of watertight doors separating one from the other. The gun barrel was sealed by a hydraulically operated tampion supposedly interlocked with the firing switch. But this failed to work on several occasions so that the shell blew off the end of the barrel as it was fired.

However, the idea of building large submarines was not confined to Britain. By 1915, Germany was suffering badly from the effects of the British blockade which prevented essential raw materials for the war reaching its ports. A first suggestion was that *U-boats* should rendezvous with neutral merchant ships out at sea and transfer cargo which could then be brought back to Germany underwater. Not surprisingly the German navy opposed this scheme pointing out that it would be virtually impossible to find conditions on the high seas when such transfers could take place and, in any case, the storage capacity of an operational U-boat was far too small to make such a plan viable.

As a result, plans were laid to build an unarmed cargo-carrying submarine which would be manned by merchant navy crew and thus be considered a merchant ship and not a warship. In the surprisingly short time of only five months, the submarine *Deutschland* was launched on March 20 1916 with a surface displacement of 1440 tons and submerged of 1800 tons. The ex-captain of the German freighter *Schleswig*, Paul Koenig, was placed in charge and, with a crew of twenty-six, sailed from Kiel on June 23 1916 for America with a cargo of dyestuffs, precious stones and mail totalling some 750 tons and worth $1.5 million.

British naval intelligence learned of the operation and, apart from making it clear that they regarded the *Deutschland* as an ordinary *U-boat* which they would attack on sight, they also set about establishing naval patrols off the American coast to catch her. However, on July 9, the *Deutschland* arrived off the port of Baltimore where its unique voyage caught the public's attention. Koenig and his crew became instant heroes despite the earlier sinking in May 1915 of the liner *Lusitania* by a *U-boat*.

Deutschland remained at Baltimore until August 2, when it

embarked on its return journey carrying 360 tons of much-needed rubber and 500 tons of nickel, tin, silver, and copper – all essential raw materials for Germany's war industry which American firms continued to supply until their entry into the war in 1917. Meanwhile the Royal Navy had mounted an intensive disinformation campaign about the size of their fleet waiting to catch the *Deutschland*. They had hoped to frighten Keonig, but, as it transpired, the heavily laden submarine made its way out of American territorial waters underwater and undetected. It then surfaced for the remainder of its slow voyage across the Atlantic finally reaching Bremen on August 2.

Although the tonnage of raw materials transported was insignificant, it had been a remarkable voyage involving 8500 miles of which 200 were submerged. But much more important was the propaganda value as the Germans were able to show the world the inability of the British to stop them. *Deutschland* was to make one further Atlantic crossing later that same year while her sister ship, the *Bremen*, was lost attempting a similar voyage. Eventually *Deutschland* was converted into a normal *U-boat* and became the *U-155* in early 1917.

But if the strategic value of the *Deutschland* was small the idea of building larger submarines fired the imagination of many designers. In Germany several large cruiser submarines were built during the war, and one 3800-ton vessel driven by steam engines and electric motors was proposed with a surface speed of 25 knots, although in the end it never got further than the design stage.

After the war, the idea gained pace of building large submarines that would effectively be underwater cruisers able to roam the oceans at will. In 1921 Britain started construction of the *X-1*,[2] a large cruiser submarine displacing 3600 tons submerged, fitted with two 5.25-inch guns in separate turrets and with a surface endurance of over 5000 miles at 18 knots (although the submerged speed and range was disappointingly low at only 18 miles at 4 knots). Despite the disproportionately high cost of over £1 million, *X-1* was a very graceful ship. Unfortunately, however, her design was ahead of current technology and after commissioning in December 1925 (only a month after the loss of *M-1*) the *X-1* was plagued with engine trouble and spent an inordinate amount of time in the dockyard.

Nevertheless the concept of a large cruiser submarine like the *X-1* with sufficient firepower to unexpectedly attack merchant ships anywhere in the world was a good one. In fact it was so good that the Admiralty became alarmed that other nations might follow suit, particularly Japan who by then was becoming an increasing menace in the Far East where Britain, because of the depression and defence cuts, was no longer able to maintain a fleet. This fear of copycat design by a potential enemy was exactly what had delayed the completion of the *M-1*. In order to avoid a repetition the Royal Navy began a deliberate policy of spreading adverse reports about the *X-1*'s abilities in the hope of dissuading the Japanese, who had a reputation for copying anything successful in the west, from building similar submarines.

The very experienced submarine expert, Commander Compton-Hall, believes that this policy of denigrating *X-1* may have worked because:

> Japan did not in the event build cruiser submarines for commerce raiding although . . . they built giants for other purposes. If indeed the Japanese had adopted the idea, such boats could have wreaked havoc in the Indian Ocean during World War II and might well have succeeded in cutting communications between Australia and the Cape [of South Africa].

These large submarines soon caught the imagination of other navies, particularly in France. French naval policy differed from that of the other great maritime powers in more quickly and fully realizing the potential of submarines. The so-called 'young school' of Admirals (*jeune école*), first led by Admiral Aube at the end of the nineteenth century, argued that the invention of the torpedo made conventional capital ships obsolete, while large submarines which could range the trade routes at will would have the benefit of destroying merchant shipping at will

17

(what Admiral Aube called *la guerre de course*), with the most obvious enemy in mind being Britain.

Submarines being cheaper to build than capital ships, it suited France because at the end of World War I her economy was financially exhausted. Having refused to ratify the 1921 Washington Naval Treaty which planned the abolition of all submarines, it embarked on building a large number of 1500-ton submarines capable of about 17 knots on the surface and with an operating range of over 10,000 miles.

In 1922, Admiral Drujon drew up plans for a fleet of seven enormous commerce-raiding submarines inspired by the *jeune école*'s thesis. Drujon's ideas were passed to a naval commission on July 7 1922, and five different versions of his plan were eventually produced before an order was placed for the first vessel on August 4 1926. Work did not, however, actually begin until July 1 1927 when Programme No. 0926 started to take shape on the slipway at Cherbourg.

Drujon chose to name this giant submarine after Robert Surcouf, a colourful French pirate who was born in St Malo in 1773. He first went to sea at the age of thirteen as a merchant sailor and became involved in the slave trade between West Africa and Mauritius. At the age of twenty-one, Surcouf was given command of the 180-ton *Emilie* and seized a number of British ships. He later turned his attentions to the Indian Ocean where, in command of the privateers *Clarisse* and *Confiance*, he wreaked havoc amongst the East Indiamen merchant ships finally capturing the 1200-ton *Kent* in 1800 with 400 passengers on board.

By the time Surcouf returned to St Malo in 1807 he was rich enough to build his own ship, the *Revenant*, and embarked on further piracy before having his ship commandeered by the governor of Mauritius. By this time he was so wealthy that he decided to retire to St Malo, creating himself a baron of the empire, and setting himself up as a godfather financing other pirates. Surcouf died in 1827 having carved himself an infamous niche in French maritime history. The French adored this unorthodox character who disobeyed orders, ended up a millionaire, and in the process trounced the British Navy.

If Surcouf was unorthodox then so too was the submarine named after him. The submarine displaced 3304 tons on the surface and 4318 tons submerged, was 361-feet long and, powered by two huge 3800-hp Sulzer diesels, had a maximum surface speed of 19 knots and at 10 knots had a range of over 10,000 miles with enough supplies for a cruise of 90 days. Submerged speed was only 8 knots with one hour's endurance which was typical of any submarine of that time.[3]

It carried an amazing range of weaponry including two 203-mm guns in a watertight turret forward of the conning tower, two 37-mm canons, two Hotchkiss machine guns, and ten torpedo tubes of which four were internally mounted for attacking submerged while the others were on a platform at the stern for use on the surface. To scout ahead in search of merchant ships, a Besson MB 411-AFN floatplane was housed in a watertight hangar immediately aft of the conning tower which, in theory, took about thirty minutes to assemble and launch and the same time to recover and stow away. To operate this complex submarine required a crew of about 130 officers and men and there was also space for forty prisoners of war from merchant ships the *Surcouf* might have sunk or captured.

Looking at the excellent cutaway model of *Surcouf* in the Musée de la Marine in Paris, one cannot help but be impressed by the size of this monster vessel. With its several decks that were not to be copied until the advent of the nuclear submarine forty years later, it was then by far the largest submarine in the world and not eclipsed until the Japanese introduced their *I-13* and *I-400* class submarines in early 1945 which displaced 4700 tons and 6500 tons respectively.

The truth was somewhat different. For all its size and complex specification, *Surcouf* suffered from being designed by committee resulting in inevitable compromises. It may have looked good on paper but in pratice performed very differently. Furthermore the design – as so often with new ideas – was far ahead of current technology with the result that *Surcouf*'s short life was bedevilled by mechanical problems. These were compounded by the fact that everything in the submarine had been specially made so it was impossible to find spares anywhere other than at her home port of Brest.

But these problems were in the future. Meanwhile, work proceeded slowly and, on November 18 1929, *Surcouf* was officially named and launched. Two weeks earlier her first commander – Captain FHR de Belot – had been appointed and by August the following year the guns had been fitted. Finally, on July 11 1931, de Belot and his crew carefully executed their first dive in the Cherbourg dockyard under the watchful eyes of the builders, after which *Surcouf* was adjusted for trim and finally handed over to the French navy. In all, it had taken nine years to get *Surcouf* from the drawing board into service.

A year later, on October 4 1932, de Belot sailed from Cherbourg on *Surcouf*'s first voyage to Casablanca, Agadir, Dakar, and Konakry returning to Cherbourg for some minor adjustments after successfully covering over 5000 miles. On September 1 1933, de Belot was replaced by Captain Leportier and for the next two years *Surcouf* made only short voyages until in 1934 it was attached to the 2nd Submarine Flotilla at Brest. In March it made a prolonged deep dive to its maximum depth of 80 metres (264 feet) with Admiral Devin, chief of the naval development staff, on board.

In August 1935, Laportier was replaced by Captain Edouard Derrien and, in November, *Surcouf* made another prestige trip to the Antilles returning via the Canary Islands to Brest in late January 1936. In 1937 there was another change of command with Captain ELF Le Gouic replacing Derrien and *Surcouf* was attached to the 5th Submarine Flotilla. A year later *Surcouf* made yet another long voyage across the Atlantic to the Caribbean returning via North Africa, by which time the vessel had covered 16,000 miles virtually all of it on the surface.

Although these journeys had provided excellent opportunities for the media to give the impression that *Surcouf* was a powerful warship ready for action, in reality they had shown up an alarming number of design faults that seriously compromised its capabilities as a fighting machine. It had soon become apparent that

20

it was cumbersome to operate, rolled alarmingly in rough seas, the diesel motors were unreliable, the insulation on the armatures of the electric motors were too fragile and continuously gave trouble, and that the design of the twin-gun turret was defective and leaked continuously. The small float plane had proved impossible to operate, because launching and recovery could only take place in flat calm otherwise the aircraft was damaged by hitting the enormous outer casing.

But the most important problem it exposed was that *Surcouf* took about 2.5 minutes to submerge to a depth of forty feet whereas conventional submarines, such as the British *U-class*, could reach the same depth from full buoyancy in around 27 seconds. This made *Surcouf* extremely vulnerable to attack from aircraft, especially as she carried no form of radar.

Underwater *Surcouf* also proved very unpredictable and with twenty-four vents to adjust buoyancy, trim was hard to set and on more than one occasion she went out of control and reached depths dangerously beyond her design limits before trim could be recovered.

Stringent financial restrictions throughout the French navy during the inter-war years prevented *Surcouf* from carrying out any manoeuvres to test its ability to intercept merchant ships on the high seas which was, of course, the sole purpose of its design. What was supposed to happen was that *Surcouf*'s float plane would be taken from its hangar, lifted into the water by a crane and would then fly off and reconnotre an area of some fifty miles radius until a suitable target was found. The aircraft would return to *Surcouf*, be lifted back on board, stowed away in its hangar, and the submarine would then steer an interception course initially on the surface (while the guns were loaded) and then dive just before the victim was sighted.

Range and bearing would be fed to the gunlayer who would elevate the guns accordingly and *Surcouf* would then rise allowing the muzzles just to break surface. The method of operating the twin 8-inch guns was particularly complicated. The muzzle of each gun was sealed with a tampion which was controlled by a complex rod-and-pinion mechanism from inside the turret. The tampion would be opened as soon as the muzzle was clear of the water, the guns would fire, the tampions would be shut, and *Surcouf* would slide back into the depths to reload the guns before making the next attack. The theory was that the merchant ship would suddenly find itself under attack from 8-inch shells apparently coming from nowhere.

On paper in the comfort of a design office all this may have sounded very easy, but in practice several things could go wrong. If the tampions were opened too soon the guns flooded and could not be used. If they were left in place when the guns were fired the end of the muzzles disappeared with the shell. Although the system was tried out during *Surcouf*'s protracted trials, it was never attempted under wartime conditions. As a result by the time war was declared in September 1939, *Surcouf*'s crew was still not properly trained, while the role for which the submarine had been designed was no longer of importance not only because the capital ship was still much in evidence, but also because most merchant ships travelled in armed convoys that could outgun *Surcouf*.

In fairness to the designers, many of the technical problems afflicting *Surcouf* were typical of the teething troubles that occur with any new warship and, had the remaining six vessels been built, doubtless most of them would have been corrected but, because *Surcouf* was already obsolescent by the time she went into service, not surprisingly nothing more was done about building any more of the class.

In March 1939, *Surcouf* went off on a voyage to North Africa. When war was declared it was ordered to sail from there to the Antilles to take part in anti-submarine patrols. By this time there were problems with the electric motors and the batteries. In addition, the hydroplanes would not work properly and the rudder mechanism was defective so, on September 12, it was decided the submarine should return to Brest for a major overhaul. On September 26, *Surcouf* sailed from Martinique and acted as escort to the British convoy KJ-2 of some twenty-six merchant ships from Jamaica to Britain. She finally reached Brest on October 19 when Le Gouic was replaced by Captain

PMH Martin and the dockyard began a major overhaul that was to last many months.

In the seven years that *Surcouf* had been in commission she had never once attempted to perform the task for which she was designed and, because of her slow submerged speed and endurance, had not taken part in any normal submarine exercises. What role the French navy thought *Surcouf* would play in the war is unknown, but as it transpired events overtook any future plans and she became enmeshed in a chain of peculiar misfortunes that was to make her the *Flying Dutchman* of the French fleet.

NOTES

1. Design details of the *M-1* can be found in ADM 138/560(374) (PRO, Kew), *M-Class Submarines*, Martin H Brice (Outline Publications, 1983), *Submarine Warfare: Monsters and Midgets*, Richard Compton-Hall (Blandford Press, 1985), and specifications and drawings kindly supplied by Vickers Shipbuilding & Engineering Limited. The log of *M-1* is in ADM 173/11205, and that for *M-2* in ADM 173/11401; the *M-1* was lost following a collision in November 1925 and details can be found in ADM 116/2292 & 2293, and *M-2* was lost in 1932 as the result of an accident and details are in ADM 8759/879 (PRO, Kew).
2. Details of the submarines *X-1* and the *Deutschland* can be found in *Submarine Warfare: Monsters and Midgets* and *Submarine Design and Development*, Norman Friedman (Naval Institute Press, Annapolis, 1983).
3. The specification of *Surcouf* and the history of her design, construction, commissioning and service with the French navy until 1939 is to be found in File TTY/683 (Vincennes Archives, Paris).

CHAPTER 3

A SHIP DIVIDED

By the spring of 1940 the war was costing Britain £6 million a day but, even after six months' hostilities, there was remarkably little to show for it. There had been some naval actions both in home waters and the South Atlantic resulting in losses of capital ships on both sides. The Germans had been forced to ignominiously scuttle the *Graf Spee*[1] after a brilliant action by Royal Navy cruisers but U-boats had torpedoed the battleship HMS *Royal Oak*[2] right inside the naval base at Scapa Flow and then the aircraft carrier HMS *Courageous*[3] off the west coast of Scotland. But in the air and on the ground little was happening and even the heavily censored jingoistic newsreels were hard pressed to show anything more than troops singing a banal song *'We're going to hang out the washing on the Ziegfried Line'*.

The Americans called it the 'Phoney War'; the French *'la drole de guerre'*; the Germans the *'sitzkrieg'*; the British the 'Bore War'; and Churchill the 'Twilight War'. As the months passed people became bored and morale slumped. The heady euphoria of the previous autumn when Britain and France had gone to war to save Poland now seemed far away. The Franco-Polish military agreement of May 19 1939 had stated that:

as soon as the principal German effort against Poland develops France will launch an offensive against

24

Germany with the bulk of her forces.[4]

This attack by *les gros de ses forces* would start on the fifteenth
day after mobilization but the French C-in-C, General Maurice
Gamelin, ingenuously claimed that *les gros* meant only certain
main units of the French army and not *le gros* – the bulk of the
army. On August 23 1939 Gamelin told his government that a
serious offensive could not be launched for at least two years
and then pointed out that the agreement between France and
Poland had not actually been signed.

Britain's attitude was no better and, although they had
assured Poland of 'immediate and full support', nothing happened other than some small shipments of military equipment
most of which were turned back before they reached Polish
ports when Poland's defeat seemed obvious. As Poland's remaining forces fought to their deaths Churchill took time off
from the War Cabinet and visited naval defences in Scotland.
On September 18 he picnicked by a sparkling stream in the
warm sunshine and contemplated the future:

> What of the supreme measureless ordeal in which we
> were again irrevocably plunged? Poland in its agony;
> France but a pale reflection of her former warlike
> ardour; the Russian colossus no longer an ally, not even
> neutral, possibly to become a foe. Italy no friend. Japan
> no ally. Would America ever come in again? The British
> Empire remained intact and gloriously united but ill-
> prepared, unready. We still had command of the sea. We
> were woefully outmatched in numbers in . . . the air.
> Somehow the light faded out of the landscape.[5]

While Churchill pondered, Hitler continued his march through
Poland with fifty-eight divisions of which fourteen were *panzers*
and within twenty-eight days it was all over. In Britain many
began to wonder whether there was much point in continuing
now that the cause for going to war was over.

The idea that a negotiated peace even at this late hour might

25

provide a welcome face-saving solution to an unnecessary war was not confined to a few pacifists.[6] A large section – indeed probably a majority – of the well-educated and wealthier upper classes had no wish to fight Hitler who many regarded as having saved Germany from communism, a greater menace than Nazism. In France there was no greater desire to fight Germany particularly as the French knew that most of it would be on their soil and they had no wish to repeat the carnage of the last war.

Even before the war had started strenuous efforts had been made in Britain to maintain contact with Hitler, one channel being through Rudolf Hess[7] who was considered to be less of a Nazi thug than the rest of his clique. In 1937 Dr Franz Gerl, a close friend of Hess, had with Hitler's approval arranged a meeting between Hess and several supposedly influential members of the British establishment including Oliver Baldwin and Lady Cripps.

In addition there was the Right Club in London, founded in May 1939, with the official aim of improving relations between Britain and Germany but in reality more concerned with whipping up anti-Semitic propaganda by claiming the Jews were responsible for the war. Others who it was alleged shared anti-war views included Queen Mary (who was German by birth) and the Duke of Windsor who with the Duchess had made a highly controversial visit to Germany in 1937 against the wishes of the British government. On several occasions the Duke had publicly declared there was no reason for the two countries to go to war.

None of this helped inspire a warlike feeling amongst the people who, apart from some vague rhetorical statements in the press, were given no idea how Britain and France intended to defeat Germany. In fact they got more news about the war by listening to Hamburg radio and the broadcasts of two renegade Englishmen, Norman Baillie-Stewart and William Joyce.[8] The latter earned the nickname Lord Haw Haw, coined by the *Daily Express* on September 14 1939, and by January 1940 the Ministry of Information estimated that 26 per cent of the population were listening to these broadcasts.

The nation was not helped by Prime Minister Neville

Chamberlain's lacklustre leadership. On September 10 1939 he privately confided in his diary:

> One thing comforts me. While war was still averted, I felt I was indispensable for no one else could carry out my policy. Today the position has changed. Half a dozen people could take my place while war is in progress, and I do not see I have any particular part to play until it comes to discussing peace terms, and that may be a long way off.

The strategic policy on which the war was to be fought had been agreed at Anglo–French talks in early 1939 and concluded that:

> We should be faced by enemies who would be more fully prepared for war than ourselves, would have superiority in air and land forces, but would be inferior at sea and in general economic strength . . . to defeat such an [enemy] our major strategy would be defensive.[9]

In reality all this meant was that nothing happened and the small British Expeditionary Force (BEF) and its much larger French allies sat in their trenches and concrete Maginot Line and waited for the enemy to attack. The government believed that the Royal Navy's blockade would soon bring the German war effort to a halt conveniently ignoring the fact that Germany was able to import all it wanted from Russia – then its ally – and through Italy and the Balkans.[10] In an effort to explain the government's intentions, the Ministry of Information issued a leaflet which said:

> We do not have to defeat the Nazis on land, but only prevent them from defeating us.

While the armies sat around in France the British people waited for the bombs to rain down on them from the hordes of German bombers that had been so confidently predicted by the experts.[11]

But again nothing happened. The only casualties were from the all-enveloping blackout that was rigorously enforced by the air-raid wardens who had nothing else to do.

To many people it did not seem as if there really was a war on. Blocks of new luxury flats and cinemas were still being built. The car industry continued to advertise its products. Race meetings adhered to their prewar calendar and courses were crammed. There still seemed to be plenty of able-bodied men standing outside hotels and stores opening taxi doors while the wealthy arrived in large cars driven by uniformed chauffeurs.

If life in Britain seemed far removed from the horrors of war then life in France was even more so. After the first heady days of excitement the French quickly lost interest. Apart from a few more uniforms on the streets, Paris remained as in peacetime. Unlike Britain the blackout was tolerated but not enforced with much vigour. Cafés and restaurants were crowded and menus had not suffered. Fashion shows continued unabated. The newspapers and newsreels carried endless stories of happy French soldiers securely entrenched in their impregnable Maginot Line[12] and much time was given to reporting the endless stream of dignitaries who visited this useless fortification, which only served to sum up the strategic thinking of France's high command.

One visitor was the Duke of Windsor, now attached to the BEF, who, after inspecting the fortifications, saw the fatal flaw in this defence system and wrote a very prescient report to the War Office in London about its shortcomings. Unfortunately because the Duke was out of favour following his abdication his report was ignored, although in fairness it is hard to see how the British could have altered French thinking.

Neither the French government nor its generals had any intention of taking the offensive along the western front, although on September 6 1939 Gamelin ordered a cautious advance some miles into undefended German territory which resulted in the 'capture' of some twenty German villages. Much was made of this in the press but thereafter the French and the BEF made no further advances for fear of upsetting the enemy. In the mean-

28

time the French war ministry was considering all manner of exotic plans including the landing of troops in Norway to aid Finland (then fighting Russia) and attacking German oil supplies passing through the Black Sea. Indeed they seemed willing to consider any harebrained scheme other than attacking Germany itself.

For the crew of the *Surcouf* the war had so far passed very peacefully. Billeted ashore in the comfortable new naval barracks at Brest there was very little for the officers and men to do and so they went home in batches on extended leave. The submarine now lay in pieces with both Sulzer engines completely stripped down and, in common with any naval dockyard around the world, the engineers seemed in no hurry to put things back together again.

The lack of urgency was surprising. In theory *Surcouf* should have been out on the high seas as part of the allied blockade busily intercepting merchant ships carrying essential war supplies for Germany. But, because *Surcouf* had never trained for this work and had anyway proved so unreliable, that role was no longer possible and the French navy had no other use for it. The dockyard staff saw no reason to rid themselves of a comfortable job that was providing ample overtime and, as *Surcouf* was a unique design, every replacement part – nut, bolt, valve, or pump – had to be made specially. As a result what would have been a simple maintenance task for any normal submarine became a major engineering headache.

The air of unreality continued. Estate agents were busily trying to find a tenant for:

the lovely historical island of Jethou in the Channel
Islands, of forty-four acres with a daily air service to
England.

The French National Tourist Office issued beguiling advertisements designed to lure British holidaymakers to their deserted lanes, uncrowded beaches, and casinos all far from thoughts of war. It all seemed to good to be true. Perhaps, as Chamberlain had told Parliament, Hitler had really 'missed the bus'. Then on April 9 1940, just as racegoers at the Grand National were enjoying themselves, Hitler invaded Norway. After considerable delay a British military force was landed to support our gallant Norwegian allies. Suddenly war seemed a lot more real and a lot closer.

Although the German navy suffered some unexpected heavy losses at the hands of Norwegian land-based gunners in the opening phases of the campaign it was the Royal Navy who were to bear the brunt of the losses. This was mainly due to the fact that the German naval intelligence service *Beobachtung-Dienst* (usually known as *B-Dienst*), had, from 1937, with the initial help of the Italians, broken all the Royal Navy's operational codes.[13] As a result they were able to anticipate many of the Admiralty's plans with disastrous results that eventually led to the ignominious evacuation of the British military force from Narvik.

Less than a fortnight later, on April 20 1940, war suddenly came to Britain. Not with mass air attacks scattering bombs and drenching towns and cities with poison gas but with a single German bomber badly off course who, chased by some defending Hurricane fighters, jettisoned its bombs near the Bridge of Wraith, on the Orkney Islands, killing James Ibister, a twenty-seven-year-old labourer. After seven months of war Britain had its first air-raid victim.

The French watched the Norwegian campaign with interest but took no part. They believed it was a pre-emptive attack by the Germans to prevent Britain from violating Norwegian neutrality. The British were attempting to blockade coastal sea routes around Norway, through which Germany was getting essential imports of iron ore, and some French observers argued that had the British press not discussed so openly the value of using Norwegian waters in this way Hitler would have been content to leave Norway alone and neutral.

This timid attitude was not peculiar to the French. In Britain, attempts to start operations that would really hurt the Nazi economy were sharply discouraged. When, for example, Leopold Amery tried to persuade Sir Kingsley Wood, the Minister for Air, to start bombing the massive Krupp factories in the heart of the Ruhr, he was told in Parliament that this could not be done because Krupp's factories were private property. Instead RAF bombers continued to deluge the German population each night with millions of leaflets containing vague exhortations against Hitler thereby consuming the paper British people were being told to save.

In truth the British and French governments' knowledge of the German war machine was virtually nonexistent. The British Secret Intelligence Service (SIS), or MI6, had no agents of any value working inside Germany. The three services each had their own intelligence agency directed against Germany: the Air Ministry's AI3(b), the War Office's MI3(b), and the Admiralty's Operational Intelligence Centre (OIC). France had much the same sort of arrangements but also knew little of what was happening inside Germany. As there was no co-operation between any of these agencies, and none between France and Britain, a great deal of time and effort was wasted duplicating identical inquiries which frequently led to internecine quarrelling.

The intelligence experts gave Germany credit for far larger and better equipped forces than it really possessed. They also had the naïve belief that if the naval blockade continued Germany's war machine would soon grind to a halt. In reality it was the invasion of Poland which had virtually exhausted Germany's army which had never been trained or equipped for a prolonged war because Hitler had not expected the participation of Britain and France. Germany's forces on the border with France were extremely light and would have been unable to survive an attack by massed allied forces.

The only area where France had an intelligence lead over Britain was in breaking the German *Enigma* code machine because it had acquired the services of a German traitor, Hans Thilo Schmidt, codenamed *Asché*, who, during the 1930s, had given them enough documentary material to enable Captain Gustave Bertrand, head of the French radio intelligence service, to begin decoding a few messages.[14] Bertrand had tried to in-

31

terest the British Government Code and Cipher School (GCCS) but was rebuffed and instead joined forces with Polish code-breakers. Only in mid-1939 did GCCS belatedly show interest in the matter and shortly before war was declared the Poles handed over their copies of *Enigma* to it together with all their expertise. By early 1940 GCCS together with the French were starting to break the few German messages being sent by radio and thus capable of interception.

Despite the heavily censored media, the fiasco of the Norwegian campaign gradually became public knowledge and as fear mounted morale sagged, finally resulting in an acrimonious debate in Parliament on May 7 and 8 1940. Under fierce attack from all sides Chamberlain faced a rebellion from his own party and the next day, May 9, announced his intention of resigning.

Chamberlain wanted his successor to be Lord Halifax and so too did King George VI, most of the Conservative party, and the Labour opposition. But amongst other reasons Halifax felt that because he was a peer and therefore unable to sit in the House of Commons he could not lead the country properly. As a result the choice fell on the maverick politician Winston Churchill who up till then had enjoyed a chequered career, having changed sides frequently and more often than not ended up in the political wilderness. Far from being the people's popular choice, as mythology would have it, Churchill came to power not by election but because a frightened nation wanted someone with charisma to save them from impending defeat. Even as Churchill accepted office on May 10 1940 he too had his doubts and remarked:

I hope that it is not too late. I am very much afraid it is. We can only do our best.[15]

As Churchill entered 10 Downing Street so the Germans unleashed their three-phase attack that was to become the battle for France. The opening phase, from May 10 to 16, included the invasion of Holland and Belgium and the fall of the supposedly impregnable fortress at Eben Emael amongst other frontier defences. British forces left their well-prepared defences and advanced north to the Meuse and Dyle rivers linking up with the Belgian army, who had not allowed them on their soil previously for fear of upsetting the Germans. It looked like a repeat of World War I with the main German thrust coming through Belgium in the north.

On paper the armies seemed evenly matched. The Germans had 138 divisions against a total allied strength of 144 divisions. But the figures were misleading. Many of the German divisions had experienced battle in Poland and knew how to use their massive tank formations and dive-bombing aircraft like the *Stuka* in close co-operation and with deadly effect. By contrast neither the British nor French armies had done any fighting at all and the BEF was very poorly equipped particularly with modern anti-tank weapons. Having drawn the BEF up to the north on May 15 German armoured divisions broke through the lightly defended French lines in the supposedly impenetrable Ardennes forests, crossed the Meuse at Sedan, and as von Runstedt's panzers raced across France to the Channel ports split the allied forces in two like a rotten apple.

If these attacks could not be contained on the battlefield the censors made sure they were kept from people back home. Casual references to strategic withdrawals served for a time to conceal the truth while the defeat of the Dutch forces was attributed to a mythical Fifth Column of traitors[16] and the surrender of Belgian forces to outright treachery. Only when it became clear that the French army was collapsing at the same rate and the much-vaunted Maginot Line had played no part in halting the German advance, did British people begin to appreciate the true superiority of the enemy.

Faraway in sunny Brest the alarm bells at last began to ring. Captain Martin and his crew knew no more about the true situation than the rest of the French people and so, when Martin was summoned to an urgent meeting at naval headquarters on June 15, he was shocked to be told that the German army was fast advancing on the port and would probably capture it within the next three days. It was essential that no French warships should find themselves trapped.

Surcouf still lay like a stranded whale with her entrails strewn around the dockyard unable to move under her own power while awaiting the arrival of essential spares. Spurred on by the dramatic news the dockyard staff together with the crew began a frantic race against time to get *Surcouf* into some sort of seaworthy condition. On May 26 British and French forces trapped in the Dunkirk bridgehead began *Operation Dynamo*[17] with the evacuation of 340,000 allied soldiers and on June 6 one hundred German divisions began a new attack on the Somme and Aisne rivers. Soon the path to Paris was wide open. Eight days later the German flag flew from the Eiffel Tower.

Throughout these long dark days Churchill had flown back and forth to France trying to galvanize her generals into activity. But it was too late and the will to fight – if it had ever existed – had vanished. On each visit Churchill found them more depressed, like a ship that had lost its rudder and was drifting inexorably on to the rocks. As the French army fell back General Weygand strongly advised the prime minister, Paul Reynaud, not to try and continue the war from North Africa. Instead Reynaud turned his eyes hopefully towards America cabling President Roosevelt on June 10 that:

> Our only chance of victory is the prompt entry of the
> United States into the war. President Roosevelt must
> realize this and accept the responsibility.

But Roosevelt could not declare war without the approval of Congress and in any case was facing an election in the autumn of 1940. His opponent Wendell Wilkie was riding high in the opinion polls on a isolationist ticket since the majority of Americans had no desire whatsoever to be drawn into another European war.[18] Roosevelt could offer the French even less than he was being asked for by Churchill who also made no secret of his wish to drag America into the war.

With no help from America forthcoming France's only alternative was to sue for peace. Churchill was forced to accept Reynaud's embarrassing request for Britain to release her from the alliance so that he could arrange an armistice.

From this funeral pyre of defeat arose one lone voice urging Frenchmen to continue the war against Germany at any cost. The call came from forty-nine-year-old General Charles de Gaulle, an outspoken and controversial officer – and also the newest and youngest general in the French army – who was disgusted by the defeatism of his senior commanders and corrupt politicians.

General Sir Edward Spears, Churchill's military representative in Paris, was so impressed by de Gaulle that he arranged for him to fly to London on June 17 where without any authority or resources he set about creating his new Free French headquarters even before the ink was dry on the armistice agreement signed on June 22 by a triumphant Hitler in the same railway carriage at Compiègne in which France had humiliated Germany at the end of World War I.

In London, de Gaulle found himself totally isolated. Churchill had told Spears to bring back as many French leaders as possible before the final collapse hoping this would include Weygand and Reynaud. Instead he was faced with this extremely tall and touchy young general[19] who had no particular love for Britain and was preparing to call himself the head of the French government in exile. Churchill had only met him for the first time on June 9, when de Gaulle had flown to London for a meeting to discuss the sending of further British reinforcements to France. Churchill had admired his spirit and determination and, as he was apparently the only senior officer prepared to continue the fight, Churchill put aside his disappointment and promised him his full support. It was a move which infuriated Lord Halifax at the Foreign Office who was still in touch with Marshal Pétain's government in Paris.

In many ways de Gaulle was very like Churchill. They each appealed for their people to make sacrifices at a time of great need. The difference was that Churchill enjoyed almost autocratic powers of legitimate office. He was backed by a parliament that had put aside its peacetime political differences to win the war and was daily giving direct strategic orders to his commanders. He was also in direct control of his most secret code-breaking organization – unknown even to most of his colleagues and military leaders. Furthermore he had direct access to the people through his radio broadcasts and endless visits around the country.

By contrast de Gaulle was an exile with no official office. He was not particularly popular with the British government who, after the armistice, distrusted all French people, yet had to rely on it for all his resources. Additionally he was actively disliked by the Americans and not well known to his own people, who he had little opportunity to speak to or meet. Not surprisingly de Gaulle suffered from an acute inferiority complex and was always quick to take offence at the slightest sign that his already weak position was under threat.

As a result, unlike Churchill with his populist behaviour and speech, de Gaulle deliberately cultivated a silent and aloof attitude. Although the relationship between these two mercurial leaders, both of whom had had to face disaster and defeat, was never to be smooth it nevertheless eventually produced the chemistry of victory in the long years ahead that made them two giants of history.

On June 18 de Gaulle awoke in his new home at 8 Seamore Grove (now Curzon Place) in London's West End and prepared to broadcast to the French people that the fight was not over and he would lead them to victory. That same morning in Brest Martin decided that *Surcouf* must sail for Britain even if repairs were still incomplete.[20] Gathering his crew and getting rid of the last dockyard worker, Martin slowly edged *Surcouf* out of the naval base on the evening tide using only his electric motors because the diesels were still being worked on by the crew. A small crowd stood on the jetty and watched this goliath of a submarine slowly disappear into the setting sun. It was the last time anyone in France was to see it.

Earlier in the morning the War Cabinet had met, chaired by Chamberlain in Churchill's absence (he was also busy writing a speech – 'this was their finest hour'). The foreign secretary,

Lord Halifax, had advised that de Gaulle's broadcast should be banned because it would upset any future relationship with Pétain and the Cabinet agreed. Churchill hearing about this decision was furious.[21] He did not like Halifax's weak attitude towards the French and had no faith in Pétain. He quickly saw to it that the Cabinet changed its mind.

De Gaulle, however, was unaware of any of this and at around 8 pm that evening arrived at Broadcasting House to make his first ever broadcast. He was met by Elizabeth Barker, an assistant with the European News Talks section, but because she had only been asked to arrange the broadcast earlier in the evening there was insufficient time to have it recorded. De Gaulle's message went out loud and clear on the 10 pm French news:

> Alleging the defeat of our armies, this government has entered into negotiations with the enemy with a view to bringing about a cessation of hostilities. It is quite true that we were, and still are, overwhelmed by the enemy ... forces both on the ground and in the air. It was the German tanks, planes, and tactics that took our leaders by surprise and brought them to their present plight.
>
> But has the last word been said? Must we abandon all hope? Is our defeat final? No! Speaking in the full knowledge of the facts I ask you to believe me when I say that the cause of France is not lost. For France is not alone! She is not alone! Behind her is a vast empire and she can make common cause with the British empire which commands the seas and is continuing the struggle.
>
> I, General de Gaulle, now in London, call on all French officers and men who are at present on British soil, or may be in the future, with or without their arms ... to get in touch with me. Whatever happens the flame of French resistance must not and shall not die.

Despite the place in history this broadcast later achieved at the time few people heard it. Few Frenchmen listened to the BBC French service and anyway France was in turmoil with the roads choked by long columns of refugees fleeing from the advancing panzers.

Certainly no one in *Surcouf* heard it. That hot summer night it was slowly making its way through the swell desperately trying to conserve the remaining power in its batteries so as to reach the safety of the British shore. Even if they had heard it the name de Gaulle would have meant nothing to them, and certainly not offered a rallying call because of the confused loyalties that existed on board.

During the years leading up to the war, France had suffered from a series of weak coalition governments that had encouraged the growth of both the communist party and fascism; the political split with *Surcouf*'s crew was typical of France itself. The ratings, particularly the engine-room staff, had strong left-wing leanings while the officers were mainly right wing to the point of being fascist. Far more important, all had families left behind in France who they quite reasonably feared might be badly treated if *Surcouf* joined the British and Frenchmen started fighting one another. If, as everyone expected, Britain was defeated, they would be treated as traitors and shot on their return to France.

On the morning of June 19 *Surcouf* was about half-way across the Channel when it was spotted by an RAF patrol, but fortunately they did not immediately attack giving Martin time to identify *Surcouf* and so continue his voyage with air cover. Throughout the day his engineers worked on the steering gear which had still been under repair when they sailed. By 2 pm, as the Cornish coast at Penzance came in sight, it was at last serviceable. When Martin ordered the port diesel engine to be started it produced clouds of black exhaust smoke; they found that three main connecting rods were broken and so it had to be shut down again.

In the middle of all this a message arrived:

All warships ordered to cease engagement. Do not obey English orders. Head for nearest French port. Long live France.

François Darlan

Because of certain peculiarities in the encoding process, and the fact that the previous day's call-sign had been used, Martin was uncertain whether it was genuine or had been sent by the Germans. He therefore decided to try and get more information while sailing slowly along the coast to the east towards Plymouth. In the meantime, his engineers had managed to get the starboard diesel working normally and, with the submarine now in better shape, Martin began to wonder if it was wise to continue for Plymouth or whether he should make instead for Casablanca or even Martinique in the French West Indies. Finally Martin got another message reading:

> Order to *Surcouf* to dock at English port.
>
> Le Franc-Guyader

Le Franc-Guyader was the C-in-C of naval forces at Brest and this satisfied Martin that he should continue on to Plymouth. Even so he was very wary of a British trap and as they approached the port had his engineers standing by to open the seacocks and scuttle the vessel if the Royal Navy tried to seize *Surcouf*.

De Gaulle also had problems. On June 19 *The Times* printed the text of his speech in full while a few French papers gave brief extracts introducing the unknown de Gaulle only as an author on tank warfare. Later in the morning the Foreign Office relayed a message to him from the French Embassy ordering de Gaulle to return to Bordeaux without delay. De Gaulle shrugged this off and went on to make a second broadcast that evening – this time recorded by the BBC[22] – in which he defiantly offered his leadership:

> I, General de Gaulle, conscious that I am speaking in the
> name of France . . . state that every Frenchman still
> bearing arms has the absolute duty to continue
> resistance. Soldiers of France, wherever you are, step
> forward!

The French government reacted four days later on June 23 by

advising de Gaulle his army career was over and inviting him to apply for his pension. A week later he received a further message ordering him to report to Toulouse military prison and face a court martial. De Gaulle replied tersely that he was not interested in their messages.

Over the next few weeks he was sentenced to four years in prison, stripped of French nationality, exiled, charged with treason, desertion, serving a foreign power, and finally sentenced to death.

Although de Gaulle showed total lack of interest in any of this, his position in London was far from secure. Halifax, Sir Alexander Cadogan, and the Foreign Office all tried to suppress his further speeches because they did not want to upset the French government while de Gaulle's rallying cry had produced very few recruits because most Frenchmen were still bewildered as to what was happening and most wanted to get back home now that the fighting had stopped.

Churchill was not interested in de Gaulle's quarrels with the Pétain government. As he put it in his 'finest hour' speech on June 18:

> What General Weygand called the Battle of France is over. I expect the Battle of Britain is about to begin.

Churchill's immediate concern was what would happen to the French navy after the armistice if it fell into German hands. The Royal Navy was already heavily stretched guarding convoys across the Atlantic and in the Mediterranean, while the new building programme was behind schedule.

The German navy had lost the *Graf Spee* in the South Atlantic, the *Scharnhorst* and *Gneisenau* had been damaged, and during the Norwegian campaign they had lost one cruiser, two light cruisers, ten destroyers, and eight submarines. Meanwhile British naval intelligence believed the new battleships *Bismarck* and *Tirpitz* would soon be ready for service.

France began the war with a navy of seven battleships, nineteen cruisers, seventy-one destroyers, and seventy-six submarines. Of the battleships two – *Strasbourg* and *Dunkerque* – had been completed in 1937–8 and three of the five older capital ships had been extensively modernized. Most of the other vessels had been built during the preceding fourteen years. In addition there were two new battleships – *Richelieu* and *Jean Bart* – nearing completion which were similar in size and firepower to Germany's *Tirpitz* and *Bismarck*.[23] The only serious shortcomings were the absence of any radar and very primitive sonar for anti-submarine warfare.

By contrast the strengths of British and German navies in September 1939 were:

	Britain	Germany
Battleships	15	4
Aircraft carriers	7	0
Heavy cruisers	15	6
Light cruisers	46	6
Destroyers	181	22
Torpedo Boats	0	20
Submarines	59	59

If the Germans could acquire any part of the French fleet, particularly the four new battleships, then – in theory – the balance of naval power would be tipped very much in their favour. Although Churchill had good reason to be alarmed in fact Hitler, who had never shown any interest in naval affairs much preferring the cut and thrust of his panzers, was only vaguely concerned that France's destroyers should not come under the control of the Royal Navy and reinforce their Atlantic convoys. Admiral Erich Raeder, C-in-C of the German navy, had no use for the French capital ships which he considered – correctly – were inferior to the latest German designs and, in any case, did not have the manpower to use them, although he thought some of the smaller warships might be useful for coastal patrols.

With France defeated Hitler assumed – not altogether unreasonably – that Britain would see no point in continuing the war so he decided to impose very lenient terms on the French under the armistice agreement signed at Compiègne on June 22 as to the future of their fleet.[24] He did not want to hurt national pride any further so the terms called for:

> The French fleet [is] . . . to be assembled in ports to be specified and is to be demobilised and disarmed under German or Italian supervision . . . The German government solemnly declares to the French government that it does not intend to use for its own purpose in the war the French fleet with the exception of those units required for coastal patrols and minesweeping.

Privately Hitler commented with remarkable prescience that it would be a good solution for everyone if the French scuttled their fleet. The French considered the armistice terms accept-able and told the British government so. But Churchill thought otherwise:

> However good his [Admiral Darlan's] intentions might be, he might be forced to resign and his place taken by another minister who would not shrink from betraying us. The most important thing would be to make certain of the two modern battleships *Richelieu* and *Jean Bart*. If those fell into the hands of the Germans they would make a very formidable line of battle when the *Bismarck* was commissioned.[25]

While this debate on the future of the French navy was taking place *Surcouf* finally arrived at Plymouth at 2 am on June 20. Plymouth, with its naval dockyard at Devonport, had been a naval base and sailors' city for generations. Untouched by the bombing that was later to destroy its heart that hot summer of 1940 it was at its best. But now it was host to a very different armada from the one Francis Drake had seen from the Hoe in 1588.

In the weeks during May and June thousands of troops and

42

civilian refugees had arrived in the port dirty and exhausted after perilous crossings as they sought to escape from the German advance. But such was the confusion that most of them had been immediately sent back to France in the belief that the battle there was far from over. Because of the strict censorship in force the authorities in Plymouth were still living in a dream world unaware of the momentous happenings forty miles away across the Channel. On June 15, the day German troops entered Paris and encircled the Maginot Line, *The Western Morning News* carried a front-page story from a senior but unidentified RAF officer who stated that 'there was no need for unwarranted alarm' and the 'the new British Expeditionary Force was bursting to get at the enemy'.

Surcouf was not alone. Admiral Cayol, with his old battleship *Paris*, had been towed across the Channel with its engines out of action, arriving crammed with refugees carrying their most treasured possessions including casks of wine and family pets. No one had any use for this redundant warship which was occupying valuable moorings. Next to arrive were the 600-ton submarines *Minerve* and *Junon*, built in 1930. Like *Surcouf*, *Minerve* had been undergoing a refit at the Cherbourg naval base and had only just managed to put to sea before the Germans entered the port. The last arrival was the destroyer *Mistral*.

Together they made a brave sight for the newsreels and on paper at any rate a useful contribution to Britain's naval forces. There was certainly no lack of goodwill shown towards the crews by local people. *The Western Morning News* started a front-page column each day in French to bring 'our gallant allies' the news from France, although sadly it was increasingly depressing and did nothing to help morale. What no one in authority knew was who the French crews were serving. Nor did the crews themselves. As members of the French navy they were still officially under the control of Admiral Darlan and, despite being in Plymouth, each ship was maintaining direct radio contact with naval headquarters in France – a point which in all the confusion had evidently not occurred to British authorities.

Having seen their country collapse in just over a month few Frenchmen believed Britain could withstand the might of the Nazi war machine and this alone was good reason for them giving up the fight. On July 1 Darlan told the American ambassador, William Bullitt, that he was:

> Certain that Great Britain would be completely
> conquered by the Germans within five weeks unless she
> surrendered sooner.[26]

Although few British seriously believed they could hold out for long if the Germans successfully mounted an invasion, unlike the French this gave them all the more reason for fighting to the bitter end, even if the means by which to do so were far from obvious.

Meanwhile, in Plymouth the first task for the authorities in Plymouth was to move the French refugees by special trains to Liverpool where they were temporarily housed at Aintree racecourse until shipping space could be found to repatriate them back to France via Casablanca. Having got rid of the civilians attention then turned to getting the French warships back into the war. For the crew of *Surcouf* their immediate task was to complete their interrupted overhaul and get this complex vessel ready for action. This presented the Devonport dockyard, already extremely busy, with a formidable task since there was not a single spare part that would fit *Surcouf* anywhere in Britain, nor were there supplies of ammunition or torpedoes that matched.[27]

Despite the war Plymouth was, as it had always been, a popular sailors' city with its many quaint and narrow streets around the port area and the famous Union Street with its multitude of clubs. There was certainly plenty to do. The Palace Theatre was showing *Caprice Parisien – A Real French Revue*, while the Alhambra in Devonport, just outside the dockyard gates, was packed out each evening for the *Follies of 1940* starring Jack Fields and Gladys Cutter. At the Royal cinema David Niven – one of Britain's new stars – and Olivia de Havilland were

44

appearing in *Raffles* while probably more to French tastes were Bing Crosby and Dorothy Lamour in *Road to Singapore* at the Hippodrome. For any Frenchman wanting to see more of the countryside the Co-operative Travel Service offered a day excursion to Penzance and Land's End complete with cream tea for 12s 6d (63p), while a romantic visit to Boscastle and the legendary castle of King Arthur at Tintagel cost only 7s 6d (37p).

Churchill and his advisers continued to exchange messages with the French government through the British ambassador and the naval mission in Bordeaux. On June 22, however, the ambassador and the mission left for Britain after which messages had to pass through Spain which caused endless delays. After the signing of the armistice there was a great deal of bitterness on the part of Churchill who made it plain that he could not believe the French government had accepted defeat so easily. This attitude, coupled with his increasing support for de Gaulle, soured what was left of any past relationship. When Pierre Laval – who was a strong supporter of co-operation with the Germans – was included in Pétain's government the last vestiges of friendship drained away and were replaced with open hostility.

Having ordered all French ships in British ports to return to France on June 24, Darlan sent further coded instructions to all his warships including those in Britain:

The demobilized warships are to stay French, under the French flag, with reduced French crews, remaining in French metropolitan or colonial ports. Secret preparations for scuttling are to be made so that an enemy or foreigner seizing a vessel shall not make use of it. Ships seeking refuge abroad are not to be used in operations of war against Germany or Italy without prior orders from the C-in-C of the French navy.

Although a copy of this message was sent to the French Embassy in London, they only passed on the first part to the Admiralty and evidently the Government Code and Cipher

School (GCCS) did not intercept and decode any of it.
By June 30 the chiefs of staff told Churchill:

> In the light of recent events we can no longer place any
> faith in French assurances nor can we be certain that any
> measures which we were given to understand the French
> would take to render their ships unserviceable . . . would
> in fact be taken. We are under no illusions . . . that
> sooner or later the Germans will employ them against
> us.[28]

Under the circumstances the chiefs of staff recommended that
the plan to seize or disable the main elements of the French fleet
at the main naval base of Mers-el-Kebir in North Africa –
Operation Catapult – should be put into effect without further
delay even though they realized that such action would alienate
the French people to the point of hostility.

On July 1 Vice Admiral Sir James Somerville, whose Force H
was to carry out this unpleasant task, sent the Admiralty a long
message assessing the situation:

> I have had further opportunity to discuss situation and
> . . . now armistice terms are known there is a distinct
> possibility of French accepting. To achieve this propose
> [Captain CS] Holland [a former naval attaché in Paris]
> signals in P/L [plain language]:
>
> *To Admiral Marcel Gensoul –*
> *The British Admiralty have sent Captain Holland to*
> *confer with you. The British Navy hopes their proposal*
> *will enable you and your glorious French navy once more*
> *to range yourself side by side with them. In these*
> *circumstances your ships would remain yours and no one*
> *need have anxiety for the future. A British fleet is at sea*
> *off Oran waiting to welcome you.*
>
> One hour after Holland enters harbour [with this
> message] Force H arrives off Oran and repeats same

46

message using signal projectors trained on as many ships as possible. This is to ensure message is received by officers and men other than French admiral. Holland [holds] strongly that offensive action on our part would immediately alienate all French wherever they are and transfer defeated ally into an active enemy . . . believe our prestige would be enhanced if we withdrew from Oran without taking offensive action. Unless their Lordships have more definite and contrary information I consider proposals merit very careful consideration.[29]

Despite this obvious plea for moderation from a very senior and experienced naval officer on the spot, the Cabinet reluctantly approved *Catapult* on July 1 knowing full well that it would prove highly distasteful to the British Navy. On July 2 the Admiralty sent Somerville the text of a message to be given to the French which pointed out that Britain had:

agreed to the French government approaching the German government only on the condition that *before* [original emphasis] an armistice was concluded the French fleet should be sent to British ports. The armistice was signed without this condition having been fulfilled and . . . from past experience there is no doubt that . . . when it suits the Germans or the Italians the ships will, without doubt, be used against us. We do not doubt Admiral Darlan's good faith but . . . the French government is now, unfortunately, in a position where it is not possible to resist German and Italian pressure.[30]

Somerville was then to present four alternatives to the French. Briefly these were that the French ships would sail to British ports and continue the fight; sail to British ports and their crews would be repatriated; sail their ships to a suitable port in the French West Indies such as Martinique; or sink their ships on the spot. If these were refused then the British Navy would use whatever force necessary to stop the ships from falling into German or Italian hands.

At 11 pm that same day Churchill cabled Somerville that:

> The War Cabinet will be impatiently awaiting news of
> *Catapult*. You are charged with one of the most
> disagreeable and difficult tasks that a British admiral has
> ever been faced with, but we have complete confidence
> in you and rely on you to carry it out relentlessly.[31]

Operation Catapult began at 7 am on the morning of July 3 when Holland arrived off Mers-el-Kebir in the destroyer HMS *Foxhound* and tried to deliver the ultimatum to Gensoul. After a long delay Gensoul refused to see him and instead sent his flag lieutenant who brought a message rejecting Somerville's demands. There then followed protracted discussions between the two parties details of which were laboriously flashed to London by radio.

During the morning they had received the first brief reports of the outcome of the operation in British ports and were initially told that one sailor and one French officer had been killed in *Surcouf*. At 5.15 pm time ran out and Somerville's Force H opened fire. Nine minutes later it was all over. Although the battlecruiser *Strasbourg* escaped and eventually reached Toulon the rest of the fleet was put out of action; the battleship *Bretagne* blew up, the battleship *Provence* had to be beached, and the *Dunkerque* ran aground. The French death toll was 1297 dead and 351 wounded.

Immediately after the operation Somerville's immediate superior Admiral Sir Dudley North, C-in-C North Atlantic, sent a surprisingly frank and critical report to the Admiralty about *Catapult*. Amongst the points he made was that all the flag officers and captains present at the briefing for the operation in HMS *Hood* at Gibraltar were opposed to the use of force and:

> opinion . . . was so strong that I felt an official protest
> should be made and I told Admiral Somerville that I was
> considering sending a separate protest . . . Somerville

48

shared my apprehensions and said the carrying out of
this operation was utterly repugnant to him . . . in spite
of the decision [to go ahead] I still hoped when it came
to the point if it was found that resistance was to be
expected there might be time for the Admiralty to cancel
the use of force but I now understand that instructions
were given . . . that the use of force was not to be
delayed.[32]

Despite North's senior position his letter was not at all well received at the Admiralty and a fortnight later on July 17 he received a very chilling reply:

The opinions of senior officers are always of value before
an operation is carried out but once the operation has
taken place Their Lordships strongly deprecate
comments on a policy which has been decided by the
Admiralty . . . [who] . . . were never under the delusion
that the French fleet would not fight in the last instance.
The contents of your letter show a most dangerous lack
of appreciation of the manner in which it is intended to
conduct the war. Their Lordships . . . are surprised that
comment of the kind received should be made.

The final sentence was added at the insistence of the First Lord
of the Admiralty, AV Alexander (a political appointment) who
said in a note on July 14:

I feel at the critical stage we have reached in our
national affairs it is of the highest importance that I may
be able to rely . . . on orders when formally given being
firmly carried out without question.

Suitably chastened, North replied on August 6 deeply regretting
that his remarks should have upset the Admiralty, adding:

My dislike of the operation arose not from any

49

sentimental attachment to our late allies, but from strong
doubts as to its effect on the course of the war . . . I can
assure Their Lordships that I am free from any such
dangerous weakness as that suggested in . . . their letter.

Churchill, who had seen the correspondence, thought otherwise
and on August 20 wrote to Alexander:

It is evident that Admiral Dudley North has not got the
root of the matter in him, and I should be very glad to
see you replace him by a more resolute and clear-sighted
officer.[33]

Churchill's message was not lost on others at the Admiralty and
showed that when it came to the conduct of the war he would
brook no interference.

Aside from these domestic problems the international effect
of the attack was threefold. Predictably it was condemned by the
French and did much to sour future relationships. It was a disaster for de Gaulle whose pleas for Frenchmen to join his cause
fell on very deaf ears after Mers-el-Kebir. The Free French in
Britain numbered less than 2000 while 32,000 asked to be repatriated back to France.

Against this, the attack had a profound effect on public
opinion at home and around the world. Despite having been
prime minister for only fifty-five days, Churchill had demonstrated that he would be utterly ruthless in achieving his aim of
ultimate victory against the Germans and, suddenly, the British
people realized they had a true leader who would pull the nation
together in a way that no one in France had managed.

Even the Viceroy of India sent a message:

You may care to know that, so far as I can judge, the
reactions of Indian public opinion and bazaars to Oran
incident have been admirable and the effect has been
very heartening. Proof of vigour and decision on our part
which it constitutes has, I think, entirely outweighed any

disposition to sympathize with the French.[34]

Leopold Amery, secretary of state at the India Office, sent it round to Churchill saying, 'This should cheer you' and Churchill scribbled tersely in the margin 'Good'.

The affair also had an important effect on the Spanish, who until then had automatically accepted the invincibility of the Germans. The message of Mers-el-Kebir was also not lost on Roosevelt who had been receiving a steady stream of gloomy messages from Joseph Kennedy, his ambassador in London, predicting Britain's defeat within a matter of weeks. It convinced Roosevelt that Britain would continue the fight – alone if necessary – for as long as it took to win and encouraged him to do all he could to help short of entering the war. Even in Germany, which with good cause was busy celebrating its incredible victory over most of Europe, it provided a salutary warning that Britain, with the extra defence of the English Channel, would not be such an easy victim.

But for the French who had made the brave decision to leave their country and come and fight with de Gaulle at a time when German victory still seemed inevitable it meant they had joined forces with a country which had French blood on its hands. Inevitably this would mean that in future they would be considered traitors by those left behind in France with all the dire consequences this might mean for their families under the pro-German Vichy regime.

NOTES

1. One of Germany's 'pocket battleships' the *Graf Spee* was engaged in commerce, raiding alone in the South Atlantic. Under her skilled captain, Hans Langsdorff, she had sunk nine merchant ships totalling 50,089 tons when on December 13 1939 she was challenged by the British cruisers *Ajax, Achilles,* and *Exeter*. The Battle of the River Plate that followed demolished the fast 'pocket battleship' philosophy for although equipped with triple 11-inch guns the *Graf Spee* could not cope with three fast-moving targets. Although she crippled the *Exeter*, the *Graf Spee* was also badly damaged and had to put into Montevideo for repairs. Political pressure by the British government forced the Uruguayans to limit the length

of time *Graf Spee* could spend in harbour by international law, while a skilful disinformation campaign mounted by naval intelligence gave the impression that the Royal Navy had a large force, including battleships, waiting outside. Hitler's lack of knowledge of naval affairs was clearly demonstrated when he ordered Langsdorff to scuttle his ship rather than surrender or be defeated in a naval battle. This he did on December 17 and then committed suicide. The wreck of *Graf Spee* was secretly bought by the British Embassy so that naval intelligence could recover the radar set and aerials.

2. On October 14 1939 Gunther Prien daringly took his *U-47* through a gap in the blockships and into the naval base at Scapa Flow and at 1.05 am torpedoed the elderly 29,150-ton battleship *Royal Oak* which blew up and capsized with the loss of 833 lives. *The Story of Scapa Flow*, Geoffrey Cousins (Muller, 1965), and *The Royal Oak Disaster*, Gerald Snyder (Kimber, 1977).

3. On September 17 1939 the 22,500-ton aircraft carrier, originally built as a battlecruiser in 1917 and converted in 1926, was torpedoed by *U-29* with the loss of over 500 of her crew including Captain W T Makeig-Jones who refused to save himself and went down with his ship saluting the flag. Shortly afterwards the Admiralty issued orders that such heroics were unnecessary and a waste of experienced officers and a loss of valuable intelligence. *War in a Stringbag*, Charles Lamb (Leo Cooper, 1988), *Sea War*, Frank Pearce (Robert Hale, 1990), and ADM 234, 66–8 (PRO, Kew).

4. *Servir*, General Maurice Gamelin (Paris, 1949), 410–29, and *Diplomatic Prelude* Sir Lewis Namier (HMSO, London, 1948), 54–7.

5. *The Second World War*, Winston Churchill (Cassell, 1948), vol 1, 386–7.

6. In recent years details of the extent of the anti-war cabal that existed in Britain in 1939–40 have come to light in a series of articles, television documentaries and books. A comprehensive account is in *Ten Days That Saved the West*, John Costello (Bantam, 1991). It is perhaps fortunate that Hitler was slow to recognize the extent of the anti-war feeling in Britain for, had he offered a firm proposal to end the war which left the British Empire intact, there seems little doubt that a majority of the cabinet would have accepted.

7. During late 1939 and 1940 MI6 learned that a spy known only as 'The Doctor' and believed to be operating from London was sending a daily summary of all important messages passing between Churchill and Roosevelt to Hess's office in Berlin. Since this leak began before Tyler Kent (the American Embassy cipher clerk convicted of espionage in mid 1940) arrived in London from Moscow it must have been another spy. This has been confirmed by Sir Dick White, the retired Director General of both MI5 and MI6, who tells the author that 'The Doctor' was never caught.

Because so few people had access to this information the most likely candidate for 'The Doctor' is the American ambassador Joseph Kennedy who was strongly anti-British and openly predicting Britain's defeat. The information was evidently sufficient to make Hess believe that a strong anti-war cabal existed in Britain and, to Churchill's embarrassment, Hess arrived in May 1941 by aircraft bringing with him a peace proposal. To this day Hess's intentions and his fate continue to intrigue historians. (London Embassy file 820.02, National Archives, Washington, DC).

8. Both were hanged in Britain after the war after having been convicted of treason.

9. *Official British War History: Grand Strategy* (HMSO, 1953), vol 2, 33.

10. Throughout the late 1930s and long into the war British governments held to the naïve belief that the economic blockade of Germany was Britain's key to victory and would soon bring Hitler to his knees. The prewar Industrial Intelligence Centre (IIC), which was supposed to monitor Germany's economic position, consistently got its facts wrong and underestimated Germany's ability to overcome the blockade and later the RAF's bombing raids. Even in late 1941 German factories were still only working one shift per day, far fewer women were employed than in Britain, and they possessed far more modern machine tools. They were producing luxury goods for the domestic market that had long disappeared in Britain. Any equipment shortages suffered by the German army were the result of bureaucratic maladministration and not of any shortage of manufacturing capacity or raw materials. Between 1939–42 RAF's Bomber Command absorbed about one-third of Britain's total industrial resources yet, as the Butt Report of August 1941 showed, navigation was so poor that only two bombers in five came within five miles of the target on full moon nights and only one in fifteen on moonless nights. As a result little or no damage was being done to the enemy's industrial capacity and British bombers had been killing Germans no faster than the Germans had been killing highly trained aircrews. The Admiralty were quick to seize on the report and argue that the same resources would have been far better spent on the Royal Navy defending the vital convoy routes. It was the shock of the Butt Report that led to the introduction of area bombing, a euphemism for dropping bombs at random over towns and cities. CAB 47/15 (PRO, Kew), *The Ultimate Enemy*, Wesley K Wark (Oxford University Press, 1986), chap 7, *The Second World War*, AJP Taylor (Hamish Hamilton, 1975), 129, *Bomber Command*, Max Hastings (Michael Joseph, 1979), chap 4, *The Royal Air Force 1939–1945*, Denis Richards (HMSO, 1953), and *The Strategic Air Offensive against Germany*, Sir Charles Webster and Noble Frankland (HMSO, 1961).

11. The threat of the bomber dominated military and political thinking throughout the 1930s, greatly helped by films like Alexander Korda's

Things to Come based on HG Wells' book which became favourite viewing for Hitler. By 1938 the Imperial Defence Committee estimated that eighteen people would be killed or injured for every ton of bombs dropped and that within the first twenty-four hours of war being declared the German Air Force would drop 3500 tons of bombs on London alone. It was confidently predicted that within the first six months of hostilities 600,000 people would have been killed and a further 1.2 million injured in London alone. Mass graves were planned at a remote place called Heathrow (now London's main airport) and the military expected 3 million refugees to flee the capital in panic. There would, they thought, be 4 million psychiatric casualties. At the end of sixty-nine months of war total casualties from 71,270 tons of bombs, shells, and rockets were 60,447 killed and 85,927 seriously injured or two casualties per ton.

12. Conceived by the War Minister, André Maginot in 1930 the government allocated the incredible sum of one billion francs (then about £25 million) to build this massive underground fortification along France's border with Germany. By the time it was completed in late 1935 it had suffered the usual defence budget overruns and had cost seven billion francs or £166 million. Its size and cost gave a totally false sense of security resulting in a commensurately less well-trained and equipped army. Unfortunately the Belgians insisted the Maginot Line should not extend along their borders for fear of upsetting the Germans and it was precisely through this unfortified area that the Germans attacked in May 1940 thus encircling the fortifications. Large parts of the Maginot Line survive to this day in their original condition and can be visited. *After the Battle* (Issue 60, 1988).

13. In 1936 Lord Mountbatten was fleet signals officer with the Mediterranean Fleet and recommended that the Royal Navy adopt the German electro-mechanical code machine called *Enigma* in place of the old-fashioned and highly vulnerable book codes that had been in use since World War I. The Admiralty rejected his proposals because senior officials disliked having such a revolutionary idea proposed by a junior officer. Even when the Royal Air Force (RAF) copied *Enigma*, calling it *Typex*, and offered machines to the Navy the idea was turned down. It was not until 1942 that the Navy admitted their codes had been compromised throughout the war and reluctantly started using *Typex*. Air 2/2720, Avia 8/355 & 8/356, and ADM 1/11770 (PRO, Kew).

14 The best known of the many cryptographs designed during inter-war years, the history of *Enigma* is well documented. Some of the best accounts are *Intercept*, Jozef Garlinski (J M Dent, 1979), *Enigma*, Wladyslaw Kozaczuk (Arms & Armour Press, 1984), *Top Secret Ultra*, Peter Calvocoressi (Cassell 1980), *The Hut Six Story*, Gordon Welchman (McGraw Hill, 1982), and *Machine Cryptography & Modern Cryptanalysis*, H Deavours & L Kruh (Artech House, USA, 1985). All these books

contain a wealth of highly technical detail showing how *Enigma* keys (rather than the machine itself) were broken. Welchman's account is particularly valuable since it is the only first-hand account of someone at GCCS during the war and its publication greatly upset the Government Communications Headquarters (GCHQ), GCCS' successor, who for some quaint reason still believe such revelations endanger Britain's security today. A very full (but as yet unpublished here) account of the French contribution is *Enigma avant Ultra*, Gilbert Bloch (Paris, 1990).

15. To his private detective Inspector Thompson, May 10 1940.

16. The term Fifth Column was invented by the nationalist general Queipo de Llano during the Spanish Civil War when he claimed that Madrid was under attack from four columns of his troops and a secret fifth column of his supporters within the city itself. During the battle for France tales of a Fifth Column spread rapidly with even people like Sir Neville Bland, the British minister in Holland, returning to London claiming he had proof that the Germans had been guided to a vital bridge by a German maid-servant working for a Dutch family while enemy parachutists had dropped disguised as nuns. In France the cry of *'nous sommes trahis'* (we are betrayed) was commonplace and even Reynaud publicly stated the Meuse bridges had been lost because of Fifth Column activity when in fact it was due to the army's incompetence. In Britain the Ministry of Information issued a leaflet stating:

> There is a Fifth Column in Britain. Anyone who thinks there isn't . . . has simply fallen into the trap laid by the Fifth Column itself. The first job of the Fifth Column is to make people believe that it does not exist.

Never had the Germans had their propaganda done for them so well and in the context of the story of the *Surcouf* it is a good example of how rumour quickly produces an information loop thus giving it a patina of authenticity. *Invasion*, Peter Fleming (Rupert Hart Davies, 1957), *The Phoney War*, ES Turner (Michael Joseph, 1961), and *Invasion Scare 1940*, Michael Glover (Leo Cooper, 1990).

17. The evacuation was organized by Vice Admiral BH Ramsay from his underground office set in the cliffs below Dover castle next door to which was the standby electricity generator in what was known as the dynamo room. Hence the title.

18. Americans felt badly let down by their allies after World War I, many of whom – including Britain – defaulted on payments for war supplies. Isolationism had its heart in the Midwest of America where immigrant families had settled after leaving war-torn Europe. The boundless fruitful lands and freedom from oppression generated a feeling widely shared across the country that America should never again become involved in foreign wars

that did not directly threaten her own sovereignty which was embodied in the 1935 Neutrality Act that specifically forbade a president from helping any belligerent.

19. *Moi, General de Gaulle*, Patrick Marnham (*The Independent Magazine*, June 9 1990).

20. Martin's report dated Toulon, December 18 1940, ref: 30063/EM, File TTY/683, Service Historique de la Marine (Vincennes Archives, Paris).

21. Churchill had even less cause to like Halifax when he later learned he had been having unauthorized contacts with the Germans via Sweden exploring the possibility of a peaceful settlement to the war.

22. After the second broadcast, Leonard Miall, head of the European News Talks sections, took de Gaulle to meet the BBC's director-general who congratulated him on his courageous stand. De Gaulle then asked if his first broadcast on the previous day had been recorded for posterity and Miall had to explain that due to lack of time it had not been possible. In those days recordings were made on wax discs and the BBC only had six recording suites for their entire domestic and overseas output which were always in great demand. De Gaulle berated the director-general for failing to appreciate the historical importance of what he had said, so it was tactfully suggested he repeated his first broadcast on June 24 which was recorded and is the only version available today. (Interview with Leonard Miall, July 7 1990).

23. *Bismarck* and *Tirpitz* were both supposed to comply with the naval treaty limitation of a maximum size of 35,000 tons but the Germans ignored this and by the time they were ready for sea they were nearly 42,000 tons, a fact British naval intelligence failed to notice. *Bismarck* sailed on her first voyage on May 18 1941 and, after sinking HMS *Hood* in a short engagement on May 24 and badly damaging HMS *Prince of Wales*, was sunk on May 27. *Tirpitz* made her first voyage on January 16 1942 to Norway where she remained a menace to British arctic convoys but never actually put to sea. After numerous attacks from submarines and aircraft *Tirpitz* was finally sunk by the RAF using 12,000 lb bombs on November 12 1944.

24. *Invasion Scare 1940*, 90

25. PREM 3/179/1 (PRO, Kew).

26. *Invasion Scare 1940*, 92

27. This was a problem that continued to affect *Surcouf*'s fighting abilities wherever she went. Fortunately, as the vessel never fired a shot in anger, replacements were not needed.

28. ADM 1/19177 (PRO, Kew).

29. ADM 1/19178 (PRO, Kew).

30. PREM 3/179/1 (PRO, Kew).

31. PREM 3/179/1, Folio 23 (PRO, Kew).

32. 'Most Secret and Personal' letter X/163/645, and the rest of the exchanges

are in ADM 1/19177 (PRO, Kew).
33. North's career was abruptly terminated and he was never heard of again.
34. PREM 3/179/1, Folio 2 (PRO, Kew).

CHAPTER 4

THE FLYING DUTCHMAN

Having sunk, immobilized or taken over the French fleet the British were then faced with the problem of what to do with the ships now under their control. The first task was create a Free French navy and, as de Gaulle had no naval experience, sixty-three-year-old Vice Admiral Emile Muselier agreed to take on this task even though he was actually senior in rank to de Gaulle.

Muselier was the only one of fifty French admirals who decided to continue the fight against the Germans, and had arrived in Britain by air from Gibraltar on June 30 1940 unaware of de Gaulle's existence or his plans.[1] Muselier at once went to the Admiralty and offered his services to the allied cause and, after being interviewed by the First Sea Lord, was asked to go and see de Gaulle and introduce himself. Like de Gaulle, Muselier was also virtually unknown to Frenchmen and had the added disadvantage of having been placed on the retired list by Darlan shortly after the start of the war. Under the circumstances his appointment added little charisma to de Gaulle's leadership nor did the pair get on well together from the start.

Muselier did not share de Gaulle's grand vision of a free France, but simply wanted to get on with fighting the Germans alongside the British. De Gaulle disliked Muselier's temperament and called him 'an insufferable meddler'. A contemporary account describes the pair as:

> Two exceptional, outstanding French military characters,
> equally determined to wipe out the humiliation of defeat,
> [but] relations could not really be settled by the
> subordination of one to the other.[2]

A further problem was that the two had totally different social
attitudes. De Gaulle was proud, aloof, reserved, and quick to
take offence if he saw his position in any way challenged. By
contrast Muselier was a talkative, jovial extrovert, one account
describing him as a:

> Mediterranean sailor who had mistaken his period. He
> would have made an outstanding admiral in the services
> of the Venetian republic. He was the kind of heavy-eyed,
> heavy-hipped Levantine one can perfectly well imagine
> doing a little belly-dancing on the table at the end of a
> drinking party.[3]

Hardly before he had started work in London, Muselier's efforts
received a severe setback with the destruction of the French
fleet at Mers-el-Kebir and the seizure of French ships in British
ports. Growing hostility between France and Britain undercut
Muselier's ambitions and the bulk of French naval personnel
interned by the British refused to serve de Gaulle and insisted
on being sent back home. There many of them would serve with
Darlan who they regarded as a hero. Inevitably this had a very
bad effect on the morale of those who had joined the Free
French navy. They found themselves regarded as renegades and
traitors and at a time when it seemed highly likely Britain would
be defeated and when they were completely cut off from and
unable to support their families in France, who might even
suffer reprisals.

Muselier did not make himself particularly popular with the
Admiralty, who had more than enough problems of their own
without having to bother about a very touchy French admiral

who was in the habit of making peremptory demands for his sailors and handful of ships. Evidently someone pointed this out to Muselier who sensibly adopted a more conciliatory attitude appreciating that:

> The British Empire was passing through extremely dangerous days and for the moment the existence or non-existence of a Free French naval force was a matter of comparatively minor importance.[4]

Unfortunately Muselier also had dangerous enemies within the Free French headquarters where intrigues and internecine quarrelling were rife as French officers struggled to maintain their status. All sorts of wild stories began circulating about Muselier's loyalty and, in late December 1940, two members of the Free French security service, Major Alain Meffre and his assistant, forged a series of documents which were passed to MI5 (Britain's internal security service).[5] They purported to show that Muselier was engaged in treasonable activities including handing over the plans of the Dakar operation to the Vichy government, and arranging the sale of *Surcouf* to Darlan.

On January 2 1941, Muselier was arrested by the police and taken to Scotland Yard for interrogation after which he was transferred to Brixton prison where, a later report recorded, he was 'abominably treated and grossly insulted'.[6] Meanwhile the Foreign Secretary, Anthony Eden, had summoned de Gaulle to his office and showed him the incriminating file of letters. De Gaulle immediately pronounced it a crude Vichy forgery intended to sow distrust amongst his Free French forces.

Eden evidently suspected the letters might not be genuine and so too did the Admiralty who believed MI5 had acted too hastily. After several days experts finally pronounced them forgeries. Muselier was eventually released from prison on January 7, and to redress matters received a fulsome apology from Eden, had lunch with Churchill, and an audience with King George VI. But great damage had been done to Muselier's reputation because, as the official report put it:

This tragic story has left its legacy. All London from fashionable hostesses to Fleet Street journalists heard rumours of Admiral Muselier's arrest. No one knew why and merely accepted it as confirming the other rumours they had heard . . . few knew of his release . . . and a feeling of doubt and distrust remains. His own sailors . . . have all heard of his arrest and a little knowledge may prove as dangerous as ever, and the discipline of the Free French forces may suffer severely. Efforts to improve the status of Admiral Muselier have received a severe setback.[7]

Meffre and his assistant were expelled from the Free French, and Meffre spent the rest of the war in detention in Britain. But Muselier remained suspicious about de Gaulle's role in the affair when he later discovered that Meffre and de Gaulle had met on December 27 1940 just before the forgeries were passed to MI5. When Meffre was later asked by de Gaulle on January 5 to explain his behaviour he casually replied:

Even if the allegations are false, at least they give us the advantage of getting rid of Muselier.[8]

The affair also had a disastrous effect on relations between the Free French navy and the Royal Navy. Quite apart from a long historical distrust of the French and the (incorrect) belief that they had let them down badly and were responsible for Britain's heavy losses at Dunkirk, the incident only reinforced the view amongst senior officers that the Free French navy was more trouble than it was worth.

With this sort of background it was hardly surprising that Muselier's navy got off to a bad start. Some of the old ships like the *Paris* were no use and had to be towed away and left to rust in a convenient backwater. The old battleship *Courbet* in Portsmouth was turned into a depot ship for collecting volunteers.

A few destroyers and several smaller submarines including *Minerve, Junon, Narval,* and *Rubis* had all been taken over without difficulty and as these were relatively modern warships could be integrated without too much difficulty. Even so the Royal Navy considered discipline and appearance in these ships to be of a very low order which was undoubtedly true.

That left just one ship – *Surcouf* – the giant white elephant now sitting in Devonport dockyard deserted and unwanted.[9]

The question of what to do about *Surcouf* was initially the responsibility of Vice Admiral Max Horton, Flag Officer (Submarines), who had his headquarters in an appartment block called 'Northways' at Swiss Cottage in north London. Horton was one of the Royal Navy's most experienced submariners and had an outstanding record as a submarine commander in World War I. In 1937 he was appointed to command the Royal Navy's reserve fleet and was largely responsible for the war-readiness of so many of the navy's older ships and reserve crews in September 1939. Between September and December 1939 Horton commanded the Northern Patrol, a motley collection of old cruisers and armed merchant ships hopefully blockading German ports, and then, in 1940, he had been placed in charge of all the Royal Navy's submarine activities.

Although experts from Devonport dockyard and other submariners had inspected *Surcouf*, Horton did not need their advice to know that the vessel was useless and had no future role in the war for all the reasons that the French themselves had already discovered. The obvious answer was to quietly tow the hull upstream to some deserted creek and forget about it.

There was however one snag. De Gaulle. In the eyes of de Gaulle *Surcouf* was a symbol of France's greatness. It was the largest submarine in the world, the most heavily armed, and wherever the vessel went it would show that France was still a major naval power and would help redress the damage done to French morale following the attack on Mers-el-Kebir. As symbolism rather than naval pragmatism governed de Gaulle's thinking this presented Churchill with a problem. On the one hand, he could easily tell de Gaulle that it was impossible to keep *Surcouf* in service because of her design problems and that would be the end of the matter. On the other, de Gaulle was easily offended and, if keeping *Surcouf* in service meant so much to his pride, then it would be simpler to let him have his way.

As a result Churchill told Horton that *Surcouf* must be kept in service, somehow a new crew had to be found, and the necessary repairs carried out to enable her to go to sea again as a fighting ship. This was easier said than done. Conventional submarines are very complex and unforgiving vessels where many things can go wrong – and often do – and if crewed by amateurs will not survive for long. *Surcouf* was a hideously complicated vessel and, with Martin and most of his crew safely on their way back to France, the only officers available were the second-in-command, Pierre Ortoli, the executive officer, Louis Blaison, second lieutenant Rosignol, and the gunnery officer André Leoquet.

Ortoli was chosen to be the new captain of *Surcouf* not because he had the most experience, but because he happened to be the second most senior officer in the Free French navy after Muselier. Ortoli was a small brash Corsican, with a particularly fiery temper that made him generally unpopular.[10] He had spent his career in the French navy as a gunnery expert. In 1931 he had been appointed to *Surcouf* to try and get the twin 8-inch guns working properly because the large turret in which they were housed leaked continuously underwater. At the time of his appointment it was assumed that a further six submarines of this class would be built and that Ortoli would be responsible for all their gunnery operations.

In 1933 (when it became clear no more of this class would be built) Ortoli had done what he could to make *Surcouf*'s guns operational, and returned to general duties as a gunnery officer with a cruiser squadron. Quite by chance in 1940, Ortoli found himself in Brest where he first met Louis Blaison and made his way to Britain to join Muselier's staff. When Martin refused to serve in *Surcouf* after the takeover, Muselier appointed Ortoli as captain although, in fact, he had no experience in commanding a conventional submarine, let alone one as complex as *Surcouf*.

By contrast, Louis Blaison, then thirty-four years old, was a quietly spoken, intensely religious, family man, who had entered naval academy in 1925 and, after serving in various warships, underwent training for submarines in 1931. By 1938, he was commanding the submarine *Sibylle* and was therefore far more knowledgeable than Ortoli.[11] Had Blaison been appointed captain instead of Ortoli many of the problems that later beset *Surcouf* would not have occurred, and certainly relations with the Royal Navy would have been far less strained.

Both Rosignol and Leoquet were experienced. Fortunately, too, a few of the engineering staff had stayed otherwise it would have been impossible to find anyone capable of operating *Surcouf*'s complex propulsion plant.

The next problem was to find a crew of over 120. Not surprisingly, any Frenchman with a knowledge of naval affairs was quickly invited to join either one of the surface ships or the few operational submarines. As a result, Ortoli was forced to recruit Frenchmen irrespective of whether they had ever seen a submarine before in their life.

One such recruit was Fernand Davoult.[12] Born in 1921 in a small village near Le Havre, Davoult was the youngest of a large peasant family of eight. He had grown up in the poor, harsh conditions typical of that era and, having left school at the age of thirteen only semi-literate, went to work in a bakery. The work was hard, the hours long, his employer unpleasant, and the pay very low. In order to break out of this cycle of poverty, Davoult was helped by his parish priest to join the French merchant navy.

In 1939, with no training at all, Davoult became a deckhand on a small tanker called the *Léon Martin* operating between North Africa and Le Havre carrying aviation gasoline. Davoult had no interest in international affairs so, one morning in September 1939, was surprised to be told that France was at war and the ship he was serving on ordered to make for Mers-el-Kebir where it should remain to await orders. Eventually the *Léon Martin* returned to Bordeaux and one day, in May 1940, a French naval officer advised the captain to make for England as the Germans were about to arrive.

Davoult's ship finally ended up in Falmouth, in Cornwall, sur-
rounded by other foreign vessels that had fled to Britain. No one
seemed very interested in the *Léon Martin* and before long there
was a shortage of food on board and no money with which to
buy fresh supplies. After the Mers-el-Kebir affair in July, a
Royal Naval team came on board and told the captain the ship
had been taken over by the British and the crew had an hour to
pack their belongings and leave.

Once ashore a French naval officer asked each one if they
wanted to stay in Britain and fight with de Gaulle or return
home to France. Davoult had never heard of de Gaulle and
opted to return home, so they were all put on a train for London
and on arrival were taken to a camp at Crystal Palace, in south
London, where there were some 1500 other Frenchmen awaiting
repatriation. Attempts continued to persuade them to stay and
one afternoon Muselier came and made a patriotic appeal. He
was drowned by catcalls from those demanding to be sent home.
Davoult then had to go into Dulwich hospital for a small operation and while there the staff were so kind to him (the first time
in his life anyone had treated him with kindness) that he
changed his mind and decided to stay in Britain and join the
Free French merchant navy.

Davoult was taken to a Free French hostel in Gordon Street,
in north London. That night there was an air raid and he was
forced to take shelter in the crypt of St Pancras church nearby.
There he met the Sykes family, who sheltered there each night,
and got talking to Mr Sykes' shy and very pretty eighteen-year-
old daughter Eileen. Next year, on August 2 1941, they were
married and have lived happily together ever since.[13]

At that time, however, Davoult badly needed money
because, since arriving in Falmouth, he had received no regular
wages. In late November 1940 an officer at the hostel told him
that if he enlisted in the Free French navy, instead of the merchant navy, he would get paid much more, and regularly, so reluctantly Davoult agreed and, after signing the necessary papers
in December, was told he was to be sent to *Surcouf* as an

apprentice torpedo engineer. The next day he was put on a train for Plymouth.

Never having seen a submarine before, when Davoult saw *Surcouf* at its berth in Devonport dockyard he was amazed by its size and huge guns. Once on board, however, he found the vessel in a state of chaos. Apart from the few members of the old crew (from before the takeover) there was a motley collection of Breton fishermen and even a few farmers who, like Davoult, knew nothing about submarines or their equipment. All wanted to get off *Surcouf* and back to their families in France as quickly as possible.

There was no loyalty towards de Gaulle who they considered a renegade against Pétain, their hero who had saved France from destruction. Much of *Surcouf*'s equipment was out of order, technical plans and manuals had been deliberately destroyed during the takeover and, because the dockyard authorities had misjudged *Surcouf*'s draft of 7.2 metres, they had berthed her in too shallow water with the result that at low tide she grounded and listed dangerously, allowing the acid to leak out of her batteries.[14]

For Davoult life on board *Surcouf* was not only bewildering but utterly miserable. It was midwinter, and a particularly cold one. There was neither heating nor hot water for showers, and sanitation facilities were minimal. The food, which was obtained from naval stores in Devonport, was very poor quality and quite alien to French tastes. Not surprisingly Davoult bitterly regretted not having joined the merchant navy. Aside from the fact that he had no mechanical training there was no one with time to spare to teach him anything about torpedoes. Salvation came in an unexpected form when Davoult, as a result of the conditions on board, developed mumps and was sent to Stonehouse hospital. While there *Surcouf* sailed and he never saw her again. It was a remarkably lucky illness that saved his life, but others were not so fortunate and were obliged to continue to serve in this unhappy ship unwillingly and with divided loyalties.

After the war Ortoli wrote:

Things were difficult at first: not that the personnel was undisciplined but they were recruited outside the submarine *milieu* and even the normal *milieu* of ships' crews. On September 15 1940 when I hoisted the colours again I only had round me a solid nucleus of naval officers and a few men. Gradually people came from all around. Most were well intentioned but not all. The mysterious *Surcouf* was a favourite subject of conversation for the little maritime world of Plymouth and the absurdest rumours were believed. I'm not sure whether a small number of men didn't come aboard because they had heard *Surcouf* would never set sail.[15]

Despite all their problems Ortoli and Blaison did their best and, on December 20 1940, *Surcouf* put to sea for the first time since her arrival six months earlier and, two days later, gingerly carried out a very slow dive so that her trim could be adjusted.

In order to prevent any further misunderstandings, Horton arranged that a British naval liaison team should be placed on board *Surcouf*. The idea of liaison teams on foreign submarines was an *ad hoc* arrangement devised by Horton when two Polish submarines escaped from the Baltic in 1939 and crossed the North Sea to Harwich on Britain's east coast. Unlike the French there was no problem getting them to serve with the Royal Navy. Quite the reverse. They were so keen to fight the Germans that it was first necessary to explain how they should operate otherwise there was a very real danger they would be sunk by either the Navy or RAF.

A liaison team normally consisted of an officer and two telegraphists who were responsible for communications, ciphers, the all-important recognition signals and ensuring that Admiralty orders were clearly understood by the French captain. They were also responsible for seeing that requests for repairs, fuel, and any other stores got passed on to the right shore department. The British Naval Liaison Officer (BNLO) sent monthly reports by mail to Horton about the capabilities and morale of the ship, and these were considered secret and not shown to either the captain or Free French naval headquarters.

The team did, however, suffer from split loyalties in the sense that although on board they were notionally under the command of the French captain, their primary loyalty lay with the Royal Navy. It was a difficult task that required considerable tact, because foreign navies seldom worked to the standards of the British, yet needed firmness if the captain was seen to be doing something contrary to Royal Navy procedures.

Surcouf's first liaison team arrived in November 1940 and consisted of Lieutenant JD 'Jimmy' Greene DSC RN, Leading Signalman Harold 'Plum' Warner, and Leading Telegraphist Bernard Gough. Horton's choice showed that, despite his belief that *Surcouf* would never be of any use, he was going to do everything possible to help Ortoli by sending him a team of very experienced submariners.

Greene was born on 21 January 1914 and joined the submarine service on September 2 1935 serving with the Far Eastern squadron in 1936.[16] Promoted to lieutenant on June 1 1937, he had joined HMS *Ursula* on July 7 1939 as executive officer under Commander GC Philips DSO RN.

Ursula was one of the new-design small *U-class* boats and distinguished itself early in the war by attacking a German cruiser for which Philips received a DSO and Greene a DSC. After leaving *Ursula* in September 1940, Greene spent a short time at the shore station HMS *Elfin* at Blyth in Northumberland before being appointed British Naval Liaison Officer (BNLO) in *Surcouf* on December 10 1940.

Warner and Gough were also chosen because of their long experience in submarines. They were also older and more mature and thus less likely to get upset by the inevitable problems of working alongside the French.

Warner was born on January 4 1902 at Wendover in Buckinghamshire, and joined the Royal Navy's training establishment HMS *Ganges* as a boy aged sixteen on March 21 1918, officially becoming a sailor on January 4 1920, when he signed an engagement for twelve years. On October 31 1922 he volunteered for submarines in which he served continuously until the end of his engagement in 1932, when he joined the Royal Fleet Reserve only to re-enlist on September 17 1939.[17] Throughout his career Warner's character and conduct was impeccable and he was the archetypical loyal, hard-working British naval rating that formed the backbone of the Royal Navy both before and during the war.

Although he came from a very ordinary background and had only enjoyed a modest education, Warner possessed great talent as an artist and whenever he had time to spare would produce remarkable pen-and-ink sketches. His extremely articulate letters to his wife Lillian also show what a perceptive person he was. For all these reasons he was an excellent choice to help Greene.

Bernard Gough was born on May 3 1908 at West Bromwich in Staffordshire and, as he was an extremely bright and clever boy at school (like Warner he spoke some French), his parents thought he should enter the legal profession. But the lure of the sea was so strong that Gough actually wanted to run away from home and join the Navy. However, commonsense prevailed and on August 9 1923 at the age of fifteen, like Warner, he too joined HMS *Ganges*, becoming a sailor on his eighteenth birthday in 1926. In October 1930 Gough volunteered for submarines and, on New Year's Day 1931, married twenty-two-year-old Lillian Waldron at Plymouth. Gough's twelve-year engagement ended in May 1938 when he joined the Royal Fleet Reserve, but in July 1939 he re-enlisted just before the outbreak of war.[18]

Gough's skill and intelligence enabled him to take a number of specialist courses in handling and maintaining a wide range of naval radio transmitters. He consistently received 'superior' rating on his conduct sheet, and during his career was awarded three Good Conduct badges making him almost unique in the submarine service. One officer wrote in his file:

Telegraphist Bernard Gough is a man of more than average intelligence who is capable of taking the initiative when occasion arises and has given satisfactory proof of his energies. Although his junior rating has precluded him being placed in charge of men, he shows a practical confidence about his work that I believe him to possess the ability to command.

Despite this excellent liaison team things did not work out as Horton had intended. The problem, ironically, was that they were far too good for *Surcouf*. Greene naturally assumed that Horton wanted *Surcouf* brought up to the same standard as a Royal Navy submarine and, as he knew Ortoli was a naval gunnery specialist with no command experience, made it plain from the start that he was most disturbed at the quality of operational efficiency and discipline on board *Surcouf*.[19] Accordingly Greene considered it would be necessary for him to impose his ideas directly on the running of the ship.

Not surprisingly this upset Ortoli. For a start he had an outsize chip on his shoulder being well aware that the British regarded *Surcouf* not as the pride of the French navy but a joke. He also knew that the deaths of Sprague, Griffiths and Webb were still fresh in people's minds and neither he nor his crew were trusted. On top of all that Ortoli bitterly resented the fact that Greene's extensive combat experience was vastly superior to his, yet was too proud to seek his advice.

Perhaps if Greene had been a little more diplomatic and not so forceful the relationship might have been better. But Greene had no time to waste on pleasantries. Submariners are strange people, living with death just around the corner and having to accept that in war a submarine with all its crew may well be lost each week. Greene saw his job as getting *Surcouf* back into the war as quickly as possible and, if in the process some French pride got trampled on, that was unimportant.

As a result, from the day Greene walked up the gangplank he and Ortoli were enemies. Coming so soon after the bloody takeover and added to the fact that most of the crew just wanted to go home, it is not hard to appreciate the abrasive environment that existed in *Surcouf* and the disastrous effect this had on morale throughout the rest of her career.

Ortoli knew Greene was writing reports about him and his

ship, which neither he nor Muselier were allowed to see. Inevitably it generated the feeling that the liaison teams were spying on them. As a result Ortoli became more secretive about his plans which in :urn made Greene and subsequent BNLOs think something sinister was afoot.

On November 30 1940 Horton issued orders for *Surcouf* to go up to the training base HMS *Titania* in the Clyde area of Scotland and begin working-up exercises:

> *Surcouf* will be transferred temporarily to the control of the 3rd Submarine Flotilla who will arrange for necessary practices including attacks and night operations. *Surcouf* will sail from Devonport when . . . gun efficiency is worked up sufficiently to provide reasonable defence.
>
> In view of circumstances which have rendered it necessary to man this submarine with many officers and ratings without previous submarine experience . . . the period of working-up shall be of sufficient duration which will enable it to proceed on service with complete confidence . . . it is not therefore intended to specify any definite period of working-up.[20]

Horton's order was optimistic for *Surcouf* was not ready to sail for the Clyde until February 1 1941 and then only spent a week on training exercises with *Titania* which, after eight months' idleness and an amateur crew, was obviously not enough to get her ready for action. The problem was that no one knew for what role *Surcouf* was training. In theory, she should have been cruising the oceans destroying German merchant ships, but her unreliability and untrained crew made that task impossible. Greene immediately realized that *Surcouf* could not be used in any theatre of war where enemy aircraft operated because of her slow diving time. In an effort to overcome this Ortoli and Blaison tried to speed up the time by taking short cuts. As Ortoli later recalled:

> Blaison suggested opening the ballasts a fraction of a

71

second (so to speak) before the central tubes. I agreed and managed to achieve our disappearance in 60 seconds. Then one day the classic error occurred: filling a stabilizing tank instead of emptying it. It was on Loch Fyne, a magnificent winter's day . . . but this fine day was nearly our last. I saw the speed and depth rising . . . when the depth was approaching 45 metres I tried to apply drag tactics. We reached a depth of 75 metres on the pressure gauge which meant our fore end [bow] was at 100 metres. But we came out of it.[21]

When Horton received Greene's report on the incident it convinced him that *Surcouf* could not operate in any European or Mediterranean theatre of war. It was therefore agreed that *Surcouf* should finish training and then be sent over to a Canadian port where she could perhaps help escort convoys part of the way across the Atlantic and where there would be no chance of air attacks. It was also hoped that *Surcouf*'s crew would feel more relaxed and happier amongst French-speaking Canadians. As it transpired this proved a dreadful mistake for many of the French Canadians were pro-Vichy with the result that *Surcouf*'s crew were bombarded with a litany of anti-de Gaulle propaganda during their many weeks of enforced idleness in Canadian ports.

But this was all in the future. On February 14 1941 Horton issued orders that *Surcouf* was to sail from the Clyde for Halifax, Nova Scotia, on February 19.[22] At 3.30 pm that cold wintry afternoon she disappeared into the gathering darkness. For the first part of the voyage *Surcouf* was escorted by the submarine HMS *Thunderbolt* and the destroyer HMS *Sunflower*, but when at 10 pm on February 20 they reached position 57°30′N 10°00′W, she continued on alone diving by day and surfacing at night.

Surcouf had been due to arrive at Halifax at midday on February 25 but in fact did not do so until March 3 because of a number of incidents during the voyage.[23] The first of these was on the day after departure. *Surcouf* came back to the surface during a storm and, as the vessel rolled and pitched heavily, one of the engineers, nineteen-year-old Henri le Bousse, fell against the rotating propeller shaft and trapped his left hand resulting in the loss of four fingers. The bad weather made it impossible to transfer le Bousse to *Sunflower*, and he had to remain on board under sedation. On February 21, while diving, *Surcouf* went out of control and reached a depth of 65 metres before she could be brought back to the surface. On February 26 an Atlantic gale forced Ortoli to change course and the submarine rolled so much that acid was spilled from the batteries giving off highly dangerous chlorine gas; water also short-circuited the main switchgear which caught fire. Ortoli's own description gives a good idea of the chaos prevailing:

> We were short of electricians . . . and baptised three young fishermen (seventeen to eighteen years old), from Breton as 'electrical helpers'. During the fire that raged in the batteries after the ship rolled gunwhales under these brave boys stopped the fire . . . tested the accumulators, repaired the insulation . . . each time one battery was restored the other threatened to catch fire and that went on all afternoon.[24]

When they finally reached Halifax and moored alongside the depot ship HMS *Forth*, Ortoli presented the dockyard with a long list of defects. He then had to go into Camp Hill hospital for a fortnight, leaving Blaison to oversee the repairs while, apart from Le Bousse,[25] another five sailors were also admitted to hospital with suspected tuberculosis.

The port of Halifax where *Surcouf* was now to be based is the largest ice-free port on the east coast of North America and the world's second largest natural harbour.[26] The creation of Halifax is credited to an Englishman, Colonel Edward Cornwallis, who entered the harbour for the first time aboard the sloop HMS *Sphinx* on July 21 1749. By July 27 the rest of his fleet, carrying 2575 men, women, and children had sailed into Chebucto Harbour (as it was known to the natives). Within a month the energetic Cornwallis had surveyed a site for a new city which he named after Montague Dunk, Earl of Halifax (Yorkshire) who was president of the quaintly named Board of Trade and Plantations.

The main purpose of developing Halifax as a colonial outpost was to protect British interests in North America, in particular access to the St Lawrence river, against the French who already occupied the fortified town of Louisbourg on what is now Cape Breton Island. As a result, Halifax became Canada's first predominantly English town and the capital of British North America's 14th Colony.

The importance of Halifax from a wartime viewpoint is its magnificent natural harbour, the entrance to which is guarded by McNab Island and Georges Island. It then decreases in width to form the Narrows, before widening out again inland to the west into the huge expanse of Bedford Basin where its unobstructed deep water makes it an ideal assembly point for Atlantic convoys.

During World War I, Halifax saw the departure of many thousands of Canadian soldiers to Europe but its use as a military port came to an abrupt end when, at 8.45 am on December 6 1917, the French steamer *Mont Blanc* laden with 2500 tons of explosives and benzine, collided with the Belgian steamer *Imo*, caught fire, and then exploded with such force that two square miles of the city were levelled, and 1650 people killed. So great was the damage that it took over twenty years for the city to fully recover from this holocaust.

In 1939 Halifax was still a small and very quiet port with a population of around 50,000 busy with its fishing industry, local agriculture, and a small Royal Canadian Navy (RCN) dockyard: the RCN at that time possessed only four warships. As soon as the war began things changed dramatically and Halifax once again became the assembly point for the Atlantic convoys bringing vital war supplies to Britain. A large Royal Naval headquarters was established at HMS *Forth* to co-ordinate the convoy movements while the RCN itself underwent a dramatic expansion programme.

By the time *Surcouf* arrived in March 1941 several other Free

French warships were already operating out of Halifax escorting convoys. In those days it was not a very lively place for a sailor out for the evening because its licensing laws prohibited the sale of liquor in bars and the only alcohol available was a brand of low-quality rum, locally known as 'screech'. It was sold by the bottle and sailors had to finish it off before returning to their ships which resulted in a considerable amount of drunkenness.

As a result, many Haligonian families (as the citizens of Halifax are known) made a special effort to entertain the French sailors in their homes and one such family was the Wallaces. Thomas Wallace was the local optician and with his wife lived in a large house at 457, Chebducto Road, in the centre of Halifax. It needed to be large because he had thirteen children including seven girls, five of whom were still single at the outbreak of war. Wallace taught himself French and regularly invited French sailors, including those from *Surcouf*, to his house to entertain them. Much later, in 1943, Wallace helped start a club on Victoria Street known as *Maison Surcouf* where the French could enjoy their own company and have dances and concerts.

In return for their hospitality, Ortoli invited Mr and Mrs Wallace and two of their daughters to have dinner on board *Surcouf*. Recalling the evening fifty years later, Ruth Wallace (now Mrs Ruth Graham) remembers how she and her sister drove with their parents down to the dockyard and saw this huge submarine lying alongside the jetty glistening in the dark:

I had on a white hat with ribbons, a sailor hat, and one of the young officers said 'You just look like one of us', and I was so pleased. My parents ate with the senior officers while my sister and I were with the cadets in another part of the ship. We were sitting there having dinner, a gorgeous meal with seven or eight courses, and these young men kept passing what I thought was water around and my sister and I kept drinking it. We were having a wonderful time although I did think the water tasted a bit peculiar, and it was only at the end of the meal when we stood up that we realized something was

75

wrong. That was our first introduction to wine because we never had anything like that at home. At the end of the meal the cadets gave us the ribbons off their hats and we kept them for years.

The Wallace girls, and others like them in Halifax, were all in great social demand but Thomas Wallace refused to allow any of his daughters to go out with the French sailors although he did allow them to be invited to his house. Fortunately, the Wallaces had a 'cute little French maid from St Pierre and Miquelon' and she went out in their place so honour – and pleasure – were satisfied.

Although *Surcouf*'s crew were well looked after in Halifax, at the same time they received a good deal of pro-Vichy propaganda claiming that everything was normal back home in France. They were led to believe that they were placing their own future and that of their families in jeopardy. Even though the expected invasion had not taken place, the war was still going very badly for Britain, so viewed from the comparative safety of Canada, the future for *Surcouf*'s crew looked bleak. Furthermore, the damage caused during the voyage had not been a very auspicious start to *Surcouf*'s new fighting career and, because new electrical spares had to be obtained from America, it was over a month before the vessel was ready for sea again during which period the crew had very little to do. Idleness in such conditions is not good for morale.

One of the strange things about *Surcouf* was that, unlike all other allied submarines, when it was in harbour the crew continued to live on board instead of taking advantage of the accommodation either in the depot ship or in barracks on land. Life on board even the best-run submarine was extremely cramped so that washing, toilet, and laundry facilities were minimal and, because it was before the era of frozen foods, meals soon became very limited when fresh supplies ran out.

In contrast when a British submarine reached port after a tour of duty the crew immediately disembarked, leaving the ship in the hands of temporary crew to attend to restocking and repairs, so that they could enjoy a well-earned rest in the more spacious accommodation of the depot ship or shore barracks with plenty of hot showers, good food, and a chance to relax, write letters, and catch up on the news.

Why *Surcouf*'s never did this is a mystery. Certainly the facilities were available for them not only in Devonport, but also Halifax and later in Bermuda. The BNLO and his two telegraphists always left the ship and lived ashore when in harbour. As a result the *Surcouf*'s crew remained cooped up in the submarine throughout their long stays. It also isolated the crew from other submariners during their stay in harbour, and this was sometimes assumed to be deliberate aloofness on their part by other sailors, thus creating an air of mystery about this unfortunate vessel that was always in trouble and did not seem wholly part of the allied war effort. Thus it was that the first stories about *Surcouf* began to circulate.

NOTES

1. *De Gaulle: The Rebel 1890–1944*, Jean Lacouture (Norton, New York, 1990), and report by Commander GK Collett RN, January 27 1941, FO 371/28452 (PRO, Kew).
2. *Ibid*, 312
3. *Ibid*, 312
4. FOR 371/28452 (PRO, Kew).
5. *De Gaulle, op. cit.* 311.
6. A handwritten comment in the margin of Collett's report signed 'J E W', FO 371/28452 (PRO, Kew). In *De Gaulle* it states, page 310, that Muselier was kept at Pentonville prison, but the Foreign Office reports say he was in Brixton.
7. FO 371/28452 (PRO, Kew).
8. *De Gaulle, op. cit.* 311.
9. The senior BNLO at Devonport, Lieutenant Commander Shelford, kept a small Royal Navy caretaker crew on *Surcouf* until September 9 1941 when Ortoli had enough men to take over their duties.
10. Interview with Lieutenant Commander Francis Boyer RN (Ret'd), Dublin, July 1990.
11. Details from Captain Blaison's file made available by the Ministère de la Défense Nationale (Militaire de la Flotte), dated January 29 1952. Blaison was posthumously awarded the *Légion d'Honneur* on March 8 1945 and the *Médaille de la Resistance* on July 13 1947.

12. Interview with Mr Fernand Davoult, Shaldon, Devon, June 1990.
13. Mr Davoult went on to serve in several other Free French submarines with great distinction and after the war came to live in Britain and subsequently became a naturalized citizen.
14. Letter from Captain Ortoli to an unidentified friend dated May 11 1960, File TTY/683 (Vincennes Archives, Paris).
15. *Ibid*.
16. Information kindly supplied by the RN Submarine Museum, Gosport. Commander Greene declined to meet the author.
17. Interview with Mr and Mrs Stanley Warner, Harold Warner's nephew, Wendover, June 1990. The Warners very kindly placed at the author's disposal all Harold Warner's naval records together with his private letters to his wife, Lillian who, sadly, died in 1989.
18. Interview with Mrs Lillian Cook (Gough's widow) and his daughter, Mrs Valerie Buckle, Bexhill on Sea, August 1990. The author is extremely grateful to the family of Bernard Gough for placing at his disposal all his naval records and personal letters.
19. Boyer interview.
20. No. 1705/SM 117 (Vincennes Archives, Paris).
21. Ortoli letter, May 11 1960.
22. No. 620 of February 14 1941 (Vincennes Archives, Paris).
23. Official report on *Surcouf*'s activities dated April 1968 (Vincennes Archives, Paris).
24. Ortoli letter, *op. cit.*
25. While recuperating from the operation on his hand at Camp Hill hospital, Le Bousse fell in love with one very pretty young nurse, eighteen-year-old Ruth Smith, who he called Sister Oot because he had difficulty in pronouncing her first name. Le Bousse spent five months at the hospital before being sent to a convalescent home in Montreal for a month. When finally discharged he returned to *Surcouf* which by that time was undergoing a refit at the Portsmouth naval yard in New Hampshire (see Chapter 5). In late December 1941, Le Bousse returned to Halifax in *Surcouf* and went back to Camp Hill hospital hoping to see Ruth again but unfortunately she was away on vacation. Some months later Ruth learned of *Surcouf*'s loss and with great sadness assumed the young sailor she had nursed had perished. In fact, in January 1942, Le Bousse had developed bronchitis and it was decided he was not fit for further service in submarines so, after a few weeks' treatment, was sent to join the French naval attaché's staff in Montreal where, in 1943, he married a local Canadian girl by whom he had two daughters. After the war Le Bousse worked at the French Embassy in Washington (both his daughters marrying Americans) and from 1967 to 1981 worked at the Ministry of Finance in Paris, before retiring to live near Brest. And so fifty years after they had first met the

author was able to track him down to his house at Le Conquet and give him a copy of the photograph of him and Sister Oot and the pair were once again able to renew their old friendship. Le Bousse's bronchitis saved his life. The author is greatly indebted to Mrs MacDonald (formerly Miss Smith) for her information and use of her photograph, and the photographs and letter from M. Le Bousse (Interview, Pictou, Nova Scotia, November 1990).

26. *Halifax: The Capital City*, Paul McCormick (Four East Publications, Nova Scotia, 1984).
27. Interview with Mrs Ruth Graham, November 1990, Halifax, Nova Scotia.

CHAPTER 5

INTO BATTLE

At 9 am on April 1 1941 – ironically April Fool's Day – *Surcouf* began her first operational duty for the Free French navy when she left Halifax, with the battleship HMS *Ramillies*, to guard the eastbound convoys HX 118 and SC 27.[1] Using a submarine to escort convoys had first been tried in 1939 on the Gibraltar route when the German battleship *Graf Spee* was at large.[2] The idea was that a submarine would be able to use her torpedoes, or in the case of *Surcouf* her 8-inch guns, against a surface raider but it was not a very realistic proposal because an enemy warship would not come within torpedo range but stand far off the convoy and shell it and, since *Surcouf* had fired neither her guns nor torpedoes since she was recommissioned, the chances of her attacking anything were extremely remote.

Unfortunately things got off to a bad start because *Ramillies* arrived at Halifax after the two convoys had sailed. As a result, not only was there initially a lack of proper escort cover, but the captain of *Ramillies* had been unable to meet with the commanders of the other escort vessels and warn them that *Surcouf* would also be part of the escort group.

Because *Surcouf* could only manage a maximum speed of 13 knots (on the surface) *Ramillies* was obliged to match this with the result that HX 118 was not sighted until the evening of April 2. Visibility was poor and it took *Ramillies* all the next day,

April 3, to round up the convoy and get it into some sort of order with *Surcouf* taking position astern. It was at this point that the first of the many rumours that were to surround *Surcouf* for the rest of her short career appeared. One version is:

> On April 1 1941, *Surcouf* left Halifax to join Convoy HX 118 outward bound for the United Kingdom. On April 10 she was unexpectedly [sic] ordered 'to proceed with utmost despatch to Devonport'. It is not known why this sudden recall was issued, but the previous day a signal was received by the Admiralty from the Polish destroyer *Piorun* reporting *Surcouf* on surface in position 53°56′N 37°22′W. As several ships in [the] convoy had been sunk the early departure fuelled rumours in naval and merchant marine circles that *Surcouf* was torpedoing ships she was supposed to be escorting.[3]

Because rumour and unsubstantiated allegation play such an important part in the history of *Surcouf*, it is worth examining this first story in detail. Freely available archival records show that, at 11.55 pm on April 8, *Surcouf* received a signal from Horton reading:

> After consultation with Admiral Muselier it has been decided that *Surcouf* should return to United Kingdom forthwith and prepare for special service abroad. *Surcouf* is to part company from convoy forthwith and proceed through position 56°N 35°W to Devonport.[4]

Captain AL Read RN, the commander of *Ramillies*, later reported:

> At 0130 on 9th April *Surcouf* was detached in accordance with Vice Admiral (S)'s [Horton's] signal. [The armed merchant cruiser] *Salopian*[5] reported later that she [*Surcouf*] came close to [Convoy] SC 27 at daylight and 'refused to answer any known challenge'. Later in day

[April 9] SS *Nerissa*[6] sighted her [*Surcouf*] and made an SSSS message ['am under attack']. I ordered *Salopian* to close [on] *Nerissa* and inform her that the submarine was friendly and she was to keep W/T [wireless transmission] silence until she [*Surcouf*] was at least 100 miles clear of the convoy.[7]

Ortoli's version of events is slightly different, and states that after meeting up with Convoy HX 118 on April 3 he escorted it without incident, except at 6.10 am on the morning of April 8 he briefly lost contact 'owing to a black night and low visibility of only 500 metres' but regained contact forty-five minutes later. The British translation of Ortoli's report says he did not receive Horton's message until the evening of April 10 but this is a typographical error because the original French version confirms it arrived late on April 8.

Ortoli continues:

At 6.50 am on April 10 met convoy [SC 27] to eastward on a NNE course. Took avoiding action so as not to overtake the convoy from behind. Passed convoy 5 miles to starboard exchanging recognition signals with escort.[8]

It is not difficult to deduce what really happened. Because of the late arrival of *Ramillies* no one, in either the convoy or escorts, had been warned that a large strange submarine, totally unlike anything in the Royal Navy, would be escorting the convoy. On three occasions while escorting the convoy *Surcouf* submerged, but her underwater speed was so slow (between 4 and 7 knots), that when she resurfaced she was always far out of station.[9] It is not hard to imagine the alarm the unexpected appearance of this huge submarine caused crews of merchant ships as they suddenly caught a brief glimpse of *Surcouf*, appearing out of the mist – as did the *Nerissa*. Naturally, they assumed they were under attack from a U-boat.

Far from being a mystery, *Surcouf*'s departure from the convoy was for a perfectly good reason, which was known to Read in *Ramillies*. *Salopian*'s claim that *Surcouf* refused to answer any known challenge, while passing Convoy SC 27, would certainly accord with *Surcouf*'s poor record of maintaining lookouts as there were several other occasions when she failed to give the correct recognition signal. When details of this incident reached the Admiralty, a report of April 27 commented:

> The adverse criticism of *Surcouf* is not unique. This vessel is apparently extremely apt to rely on her unique appearance to establish identity rather than carry out the procedure laid down.[10]

As to the frequently repeated claim that *Surcouf* torpedoed some of the ships in Convoys HX 118 or SC 27, the facts are as follows. First, the Polish destroyer *Piorun* did not join the convoy until 2.45 pm on the afternoon of April 12, three days after *Surcouf* had left it. Second, if *Piorun* had suspected something was amiss, she would not have broken radio silence and contacted the Admiralty in London direct, but made a visual signal to the escort leader. Third, the convoy log makes no mention of any signal having been received from *Piorun* about *Surcouf* or any other matter. And fourth, no merchant ships were lost from either convoy. Two steamers did drop out of the Convoy HX 118, the *Narragansett* at 6.30 pm on April 2, and the *Lulworth Hill* at 6 am on the morning of April 7, but the former rejoined on April 12 while the latter must have made her own way to Britain because she was not sunk until a year later in another convoy on March 19 1943.

Once in British waters the merchant ships split up and went to different ports to discharge their cargoes and, therefore, one can well understand that at the end of a hazardous voyage, during which sailors have seen colleagues in other ships disappear, when they are safe in port and the gossip and beer flow, such lurid tales about *Surcouf* would find a ready ear and soon multiply according to the prejudices of the audience.

About fifteen days before *Surcouf* left Halifax to escort HX 118 her crew had been told by sailors from the depot ship *Forth*, and civilians in Halifax, that they would not be escorting any convoys but would return at once to Devonport where *Surcouf* would be disarmed because the Admiralty had no further use for her. Naval intelligence spent a great deal of time trying to track down the source of this story and, as late as July 1941, Rear Admiral PW Nelles of the Royal Canadian Navy in Ottawa, was still sending secret messages to London about his investigations, finally concluding the rumours were based on wishful thinking about this ill-fated vessel.[11]

At the time the island of Malta in the Mediterranean was under siege from the Germans and Italians who, having air superiority in the area, made it very difficult for the Navy to get convoys through with essential supplies. The idea was put forward that *Surcouf* should be converted into a cargo-carrying submarine by removing her large gun turret which, with the aircraft hangar, could provide extra space for stores. Horton examined the proposal but was not impressed; nor was Ortoli who commented:

> For the mission initially anticipated for Malta, given the time of year (May–June) and the maximum operational charge of the [electric] motors we could not be certain of being able to sail from Gibraltar to Malta submerged by day and on the surface by night. We would probably have had to travel on the surface for part of the day in order to recharge the batteries.[12]

Muselier strongly opposed the idea arguing that any such conversion would have an adverse effect on the morale of his men who took great pride in the ship, which shows how out of touch he was with the true situation in *Surcouf*. In fact, had *Surcouf* got anywhere near North Africa, if it was not destroyed by the German air force, it is more than likely the crew would have defected to Oran then under Vichy control.

Unaware of the rumours circulating about its alleged treachery, *Surcouf* continued its voyage back to Plymouth and, at 8.45 am on April 14 in the Western Approaches, was challenged by an aircraft from RAF Coastal Command. *Surcouf* failed to use the correct identification signal but fortunately the pilot recognized her and did not attack. Greene made a report about the incident and, on May 3, Horton sent Ortoli a stinging rebuke and told him to make sure he and his officers understood the correct procedures.[13] Coming so soon after the *Salopian* incident it shows how poor *Surcouf*'s watchkeeping was.

Surcouf finally reached Plymouth on April 17 once more presenting Horton with the problem of what to do with this troublesome vessel. But first he had to deal with a far more pressing and unpleasant matter. By the time *Surcouf* got back to Plymouth Ortoli and Greene were not on speaking terms. What Greene thought about the vessel and its crew is recorded in the regular monthly reports he sent back to Horton, but unfortunately these cannot now be found. Nevertheless one can guess that the series of disasters that had occurred ever since he became BNLO had resulted in some very frank, and doubtless forceful, comments about Ortoli's abilities as a submarine commander. What *is* known is that on arrival Ortoli ordered Greene off *Surcouf* and told him if he tried to return he would be shot.

After the war Ortoli explained:

I had one incident with my first liaison officer . . . after a certain number of casual incidents I felt compelled to ask him: 'When you are on board do you consider yourself to be under my orders?' He [Greene] hesitated and said: 'No sir'. I then mentioned to him the reasons which in my opinion produced this insubordination adding: 'Very well, we arrive tomorrow morning and you will disembark'. He replied: 'But sir, you can't do that.' 'I can and I am,' I replied and the next day we arrived at Plymouth and he was the first to cross the gangplank with his luggage.[14]

Plainly this is only a small part of the story since Ortoli knew perfectly well that the BNLO and his team were ultimately answerable to the Royal Navy.

85

Horton now had two problems. A useless submarine, and an extremely touchy and incompetent captain. Had he wanted, Horton could have insisted Greene return, but Greene was only too happy to be rid of *Surcouf*. As his replacement, Horton chose another very experienced submariner – Francis Boyer – who had already served in the French submarine *Sfax* during the Norwegian campaign.

Boyer was born on Christmas Day 1915 at Waterloo in Lancashire, the youngest of four children, having an older brother and two sisters. His father was an artist, but most of his family had emigrated to Argentina where they had made their fortunes.[15] In 1933, Boyer joined the McAndle Shipping Line as a cadet and, four years later, joined the Royal Naval Reserve (RNR). His first period of part-time training with the RNR was in HMS *Escort* protecting British shipping during the Spanish Civil War.

On May 2 1938, Boyer applied to transfer from the RNR to the Royal Navy and was accepted with the rank of sublieutenant. Boyer was then asked what he would like to specialize in and gave navigation, hydrographic surveying, and submarines as his three choices. Promoted lieutenant in June 1939, on January 8 1940 Boyer was sent to HMS *Dolphin*, the submarine depot in Gosport, for a training course and, on February 24, joined his first submarine HMS *H-50*. After serving on several other submarines, including *Sfax* because he spoke perfect French, by April 1941 Boyer was serving as spare crew at the shore station HMS *Ambrose* at Dundee, when he was told to report to Horton at 'Northways' in London.

It was a daunting experience for a junior officer like Boyer but he found Horton most charming:

> You could always tell how well regarded you were by Max because if you were fairly popular with him he would offer you a cigarette, if you were mad popular with him he would give you a glass of sherry. So if you didn't get a cigarette you knew you were in the doghouse.[16]

On this occasion Boyer got a cigarette, and Horton proceeded to tell him all about *Surcouf* including the disastrous takeover the year before. Horton said the vessel was being kept in service against his better judgement, but that was a political decision he had to live with. He did not know what to do with her, however, because of her technical limitations. He told Boyer that he was impressed by his period in *Sfax*, and went on to explain the embarrassing situation that had arisen between Ortoli and Greene. Boyer was then asked to join *Surcouf* as BNLO to try and sort things out, although it was politely added that if he did not want to go it would be quite understood and the refusal would not prejudice his future career. Boyer naturally had to accept and, a few days later, in late April 1941, arrived at Devonport where his first task was to meet Greene and discuss his experiences. Greene said his life in *Surcouf* had been dreadful, and he had found it impossible to get Ortoli to accept any advice despite the fact that he obviously did not have the experience to command such a complex vessel.

On board Boyer introduced himself to Ortoli and Blaison, and then met his two assistants Gough and Warner. He found the crew busy disembarking all the 8-inch ammunition and torpedoes in readiness for the planned conversion to a cargo-carrying submarine. Shortly afterwards, when the idea was abandoned, the crew had to bring them all back on board again. Ortoli went out of his way to be friendly to Boyer and no mention was ever made of his unfortunate relationship with Greene or the manner of his departure, nor did Ortoli ever ask Boyer if he considered himself to be under his command.

During the next few nights Plymouth was subjected to a series of very heavy air raids which not only destroyed the centre of the city, but considerably damaged the dockyard. Quartermaster Pierre Turin-Turin from the *Surcouf* was killed in a raid on Union Street, while the submarine itself sustained some slight damage with one member of the crew killed and six injured. During the raid on April 23 the Besson aircraft (which had been on board all the time but never used) was damaged and, although RAF Mount Batten were asked to repair it, this proved impossible and it was never returned to *Surcouf*. This meant that her pilot, Sergeant Jacques Hazard of the French Air Force, no longer had any work to do so he was transferred to No. 10 Squadron, Royal Australian Air Force (RAAF), which was based at Pembroke Docks at Plymouth, flying *Sunderland* flying boats on anti-submarine patrols.[17]

The casualties and increased danger from the air raids compounded the crew's misery for, though home was only forty miles away, never had they felt more isolated from their families from whom they were getting no news. Blaison had written several times to his wife Thérèse and daughter Francine, whose lives were complicated by the fact that they were living in Alsace (in German-occupied France) with his brother, Pierre Blaison.[18] Pierre owned a factory producing electrical equipment which he was now busily selling to the German army. Blaison knew that his letters would be read by the Germans before his wife received them, so he had to content himself with personal matters, in particular explaining his anguish over having left them, but repeatedly asking his wife to forgive him and try and understand the cause he believed in. Blaison was also very worried about getting money to his family, and concerned to know whether any reprisals were being taken against them.

On May 2 1941, while in Plymouth, Blaison sat down to write two letters. The first to his wife was full of bitterness against those politicians who had given up the fight so easily and were now working with the Germans:

> I never swore I'd be faithful to this sort of honour upon receiving my sword from the navy school. I can tell you I'll always be fighting against our enemies and only against them. We got a wreck and turned it into a ship again and we dip the French flag every morning and every evening. We've got men who lost everything . . . some of them never saw a ship and we turn them into sailors.
>
> I don't know what the consequences of my behaviour will be, whatever they are I'm waiting for them. I

wouldn't like to bring you misfortune either but I know that returning to France would have been against my conscience . . . [and] . . . sooner or later you would not have respected me any more.

Blaison's second letter was to his little daughter Francine who had just taken her first Communion. Blaison had always hoped to be there with her mother at her side, but now he was far away – an exile. Instead he wrote her advice on how she should grow up. He concluded:

My little Francine, I kiss you very tenderly. My heart is very sad and your father is counting a lot on his little girl's prayers to remain strong and brave. You won't understand this letter too well. I'll explain it to you later.

They were never to see each other again.[19]

Boyer made several further visits to 'Northways' to see Horton's chief of staff, Captain Donald MacIntyre RN DSO DSC, and discuss what to do with *Surcouf*. Having abandoned the Malta project (using *Surcouf* as a cargo-carrying submarine), it was decided to send her to the South Atlantic where a number of German surface raiders were wreaking havoc sinking allied merchant ships; it was just possible *Surcouf* might be able to catch one and with her superior firepower sink it. Another advantage with being in the South Atlantic – apart from being far away from Britain – was that the question of air attack was nonexistent and thus *Surcouf* could spend most of its time on the surface.

Accordingly, on April 24, the Admiralty signalled Admiral Sir Charles Kennedy-Purvis, C-in-C America & West Indies Station at HMS *Malabar* in Bermuda:

After arrival on your station, *Surcouf* is allocated to you for operations against enemy supply ships and raiders. It is intended she should normally operate from Bermuda but could fuel from Gibraltar or Freetown as desired. It is expected *Surcouf* will be ready to leave UK on May 10. *Surcouf* will be borne on the books of HMS *Malabar* as an independent command.[20]

When Ortoli was told of his new duties, he sent a very qualified message to Muselier:

I estimate that *Surcouf* is perfectly qualified for the mission of long duration foreseen. Such mission can be assumed in a usual manner only if this ship has got the spare crew who are to be used as help and spare hand. Almost the whole lot of this crew is now missing, that is to say, that one PO [petty officer] and three quartermasters and two engineers are badly needed. It would be most desirable that *Surcouf* could find these men at her arrival in future base for immediate replacing of the certain losses of the voyage. Estimate can stay at sea thirty days.[21]

A copy of this message also went to Horton, who made no reply, and there is no record of Muselier having done so either. Clearly the idea of providing a spare crew for *Surcouf* was out of the question considering it had been barely possible to recruit the existing one.

What is noteworthy about this message is that it highlights the significant difference between what Ortoli was saying secretly to Muselier and what was subsequently to appear in his official reports about *Surcouf*. These latter documents gave a glowing picture of *Surcouf*'s fighting capabilities, always stressing the high state of morale, the competence of her crew, and the friendly relations that existed between the French and the British liaison team. One such report reached Horton in July 1941 and on July 16 he replied to Captain Moret, Muselier's chief of staff:

I am grateful for the chance to read the most interesting letter from the Commanding Officer of *Surcouf* which reveals clearly the fine spirit of his officer [Ortoli] and has entirely reassured me about the crew.[22]

In view of what Horton had already said about Ortoli and his ship to Boyer, and what he was to say in a few months' time, it is clear Horton was not at all reassured and was merely being diplomatic.

On May 14 1941, C-in-C Plymouth issued instructions for *Surcouf*'s voyage to Bermuda:

> Being in all respects ready for war, French S/M *Surcouf* is to leave Plymouth passing the gate at 2130/May 14, for patrol within 150 miles of 035°N 040°W for as long as endurance permits, thence to Bermuda. You are to use your discretion as to modifying these sailing orders for the safety of the ship under your command.[23]

Surcouf left Plymouth at 9.30 am, escorted for the first stage of the voyage by HMS *Wild Swan* but, at 49°45'N 04°27'W, she was

left to proceed on her own, diving by day and surfacing only at night. Unfortunately, *Surcouf* had only taken on enough food for the direct passage so supplies soon ran out and for nearly three weeks everyone on board lived on bread, jam, and sardines.[24] The only consolation was plenty of red wine which was kept in a large tank and about the only item on the submarine that was always in working order.

Towards the end of the voyage, when *Surcouf* was to the south and west of Bermuda, Ortoli spotted an American task force comprising the aircraft carrier USS *Wasp*, the heavy cruiser USS *Quincy*, and escorting destroyers. He decided this would be a good opportunity to practise an underwater attack on them. Boyer was appalled because, even though America was not at war, if they picked up *Surcouf* on their sonar they would immediately assume they were under attack and almost certainly defend with depth charges. Fortunately Ortoli made such a mess of the attack that *Surcouf* never got close to the

American warships, but Boyer considered it was an act of crass stupidity that had endangered the entire crew. He decided not to say anything further to Ortoli but advise Horton in his next report.

Surcouf finally arrived at Bermuda on June 14 1941. Compared with drab, blacked-out, rationed Britain, the little volcanic island, shaped like a fish-hook and only nineteen square miles in size, was a dream world, 3500 miles from London but only 770 miles from New York. There was no holiday industry then and much of Bermuda was just lush farmland, years later to be sold to property developers for many millions of dollars an acre. There were hardly any cars and no metalled roads. People got about either by ferry, bicycle, horse and cart, or the narrow-gauge railway that ran from the capital, Hamilton, leisurely along the coast to Ireland Island where the Royal Dockyard was located.

Bermuda was one of the British colonies on which, in 1940, Churchill agreed to let the Americans establish military bases, in return for the fifty old US Navy destroyers he so badly needed to bolster the Royal Navy and protect the vital Atlantic convoys. Churchill got the worst of the deal: the destroyers were so old that by the end of 1941 only twenty-three were in service. Meanwhile, the Americans had descended upon Bermuda in force and built a huge air base[25] at St George's at the eastern end of the island as well as a flying boat base on Darrell Island.

This sudden influx of Americans with their lavish and profligate lifestyle completely revolutionized Bermuda's economy, played havoc with its labour force, and introduced unheard-of luxuries long since vanished from British shops. For *Surcouf*'s crew the sight of so much beauty, food, fresh fruit, golden beaches, gentle breezes, and warm seas provided wonderful rest and relaxation after an arduous voyage.

Aside from its importance as a military base, Bermuda was also the centre for censoring all air mail passing between Europe and North and South America as the Pan American Clipper flying boats used the island as a convenient refuelling point. All the bags of mail were taken off the aircraft and suspect letters carefully opened and copied before being resealed and, as a result of these activities, several German spies in America were detected. The main censorship office was located at the Princess Hotel in Hamilton, under the control of Harford Montgomery Hyde, military liaison and censorship security officer. He reported directly to Sir William Stephenson at the British Security Co-ordination (BSC) offices in New York, which was the cover name for Britain's MI6's operations in America (whose cable address was 'Intrepid, New York)'.[26]

The naval shore station, HMS *Malabar*, immediately offered very comfortable accommodation to all *Surcouf*'s crew but, as in the past, Ortoli refused and his 130 men continued living on board. Since the submarine was not air-conditioned, this must have been extremely unpleasant. By this time *Surcouf* was filthy, not helped by the fact that someone during the trials in Scotland had given the ship a dog which no one was prepared to look after or keep clean. A further cause for discontent was that *Surcouf*'s crew, being mainly French peasants, disliked the American-style food in Bermuda. They could of course go ashore in the evening, but it was a long way to Hamilton from the dockyard, their pay was far below even the rates of British sailors, and prices in Bermuda were not cheap.

By contrast Boyer accepted an invitation to stay with the head of the naval air station, while Gough and Warner found very comfortable accommodation in a house called 'Benker', just behind the Botanical Gardens on South Court Avenue, in Paget and owned by Mr and Mrs Baker.[27] For them life could not have been more pleasant. 'Spud' Baker, who had injured his legs during World War I, was a warder at the prison on Ireland Island to which he used to travel each morning by the Lower Ferry, while his wife Rose was a renowned cook. Two boys who lived across the road – Herbert Tatum and Whitey Froud – used to run errands and do odd jobs for Mrs Baker in the sure knowledge she would reward them with a cake or some home-baked bread. 'Benker' was set in a large garden and in those days it was possible to walk through the rear of the garden and down to the beach. One can easily understand how fond Gough and Warner

93

grew of the Bakers, and what a contrast life at 'Benker' must have been from that on board *Surcouf*.

Boyer had written his first report while at sea and now wrote a second, equally critical of Ortoli, and mailed both off to Horton. Unfortunately, as with Greene's, none of Boyer's reports appears to have survived.

Surcouf remained in Bermuda for about three weeks during which time it became apparent she needed a complete overhaul. The naval dockyard could only handle small repairs and was not equipped to handle a conventional submarine let alone a monster like *Surcouf*. After a flurry of telegrams between Bermuda and London, on July 3, the Admiralty signalled the British Advisory Repair Mission (BARM) in Washington:

> Free French submarine *Surcouf* requires docking and refit principally electrical items concerned. Estimated time required one month of which ten days will be in dock. Request US authorities if this submarine can be taken in hand and that yard for refit nominated. *Surcouf* will be available about the end of July.[28]

The chief of naval operations in Washington sent the commandant of the US Navy Yard in Portsmouth, New Hampshire, a memorandum on July 16 stating that 'Request Number 161' – by which *Surcouf* was known – was to be given priority dockyard facilities (or what the Americans termed a 'not to delay' basis) ahead of new US Navy submarine construction.[29]

Meanwhile, on June 30 1941, *Surcouf* set off on its first patrol leaving Ireland Island at 7.30 am with both motors working at 220 rpm giving a surface speed of 13 knots.[30] The object was to intercept enemy raiders and supply ships, but the voyage proved a disaster. Between July 3 and 19 there were three major electrical faults, including a fire in the main switchgear control room, putting both motors in turn out of action for several hours and leaving *Surcouf* stranded on the surface and unable to dive.

Then, on July 18, the submarine dived with the main conning tower hatch open. Water poured down into the control room and on to the batteries producing clouds of lethal chlorine gas. The main lighting went out leaving the ship with only emergency lights and, in the chaos that ensued, Ortoli gave orders to blow main ballast, but unfortunately without first closing the main air vents thus wasting most of the high-pressure air on board.[31]

Surcouf went on down out of control until the depth gauges showed 35 metres, causing the gun turret to leak badly. With considerable effort the submarine was brought back to the surface, and gradually the chlorine was cleared, but the vessel could not dive again because the batteries were now out of order. After a brief radio exchange with *Malabar*, *Surcouf* limped back to Bermuda arriving at the dockyard at 8 am on July 20.

Several of the crew had to go into hospital, a quartermaster was sentenced to sixty days' imprisonment for insubordination, and fourteen other members of the crew were charged with various breaches of discipline. However, in his official report to the Admiralty, Ortoli blandly commented:

> The general state of health seemed to undergo a slight falling off. The crew seemed to be more tried (*éprouvé*) by this cruise than the previous one.[32]

Surcouf remained in Bermuda until July 25 when she sailed – alone and on the surface, unable to dive – for Portsmouth, New Hampshire, to undergo repairs, arriving there on July 28.

The Portsmouth navy yard was a vast submarine building and repair complex and, apart from *Surcouf*, there were the British submarines HMS *Truant*, HMS *Pandora*, HMS *Parthian*, and one *River-class* submarine together with at least fifty American submarines, some under construction and others undergoing repairs. With America on the verge of war, and the US Navy feverishly occupied in getting every available ship into fighting trim, dry dock facilities were at a premium and desperately needed for their own submarines. Nevertheless, the Americans very obligingly gave up Dry Dock No. 2 (Docking Order No. 507) to accommodate *Surcouf*.

A list of *Surcouf*'s repairs was prepared by the Portsmouth yard based on Ortoli's defect list that he had sent BARM from Bermuda. It filled six pages of typescript and covered over seventy items. Some of these were relatively simple, for example, no. 21 called for the replacement of all the controls and electrical wiring in the galley. Others, however, were major items including stripping down both 8-inch gun mechanisms, changing the pistons in the two main Sulzer diesels, fitting new main batteries, replacing and rewiring the main electrical circuits, stripping out the entire telemotor system, repairing all the ballast tanks, air vents, and kingston valves, hydroplanes, rudder gear, and making all the hatches watertight.

Effectively *Surcouf* was to be given a total refit and, on 12 August, the yard estimated the work would cost $800,000 (then worth about £200,000 and nearer £2.5 million today).[33] It was considerably more than *Surcouf* had originally cost. A further $10,000 was allocated to cover the cost of reconditioning *Surcouf*'s ammunition. All this was to be paid for under the Anglo–American Lend-Lease agreement that had come into force in March 1941.

The first meeting between Blaison, members of BARM, and the dockyard took place at 8 am on August 5 when it soon became clear that the work would take much longer than planned and that three American submarines, the USS *Mackerel*, *Gar*, and *Grayling* would not be able to use the dry dock as had been originally intended.[34] Blaison then unexpectedly produced a second defect list, almost as long as the first, which amongst other items included a request for twenty tables and 120 chairs, a potato peeler, eighty-five new mattresses, and a suitable outboard motor boat.

Almost immediately two problems developed. First, the American dockyard workers complained bitterly to Boyer about the filthy state of *Surcouf*, and eventually special bonus payments had to be made before they would enter the submarine and start clearing up the mess.[35] Second, as no plans of the submarine were available the yard realized they would have to produce their own – a time-consuming chore – added to which all spares had to be specially made to unfamiliar standards in the workshops, copied from the defective items. None of this was helped by the fact that many of the French technical terms were incomprehensible to the Americans.

Removing *Surcouf*'s batteries was a major task and Norman Holt, a dockyard engineer working on *Surcouf* at the time, recalls how each set of batteries was on its own trolley in the bilges and had to be pushed along rails to a hatch and then lifted out by a crane.[36] Although this made maintenance easier, putting such large lead-acid batteries on movable trolleys was a dangerous design feature making them unstable in rough weather and the cause of many electrical disasters.

The area around Portsmouth was a stronghold of isolationism which was anxious to keep America out of any foreign war at all costs. There was also an active pro-Vichy movement who regarded de Gaulle as a traitor. Their attitude was reinforced by the fact that Roosevelt also distrusted de Gaulle. Not surprisingly the *Surcouf*'s crew were the targets of a good deal of propaganda which increased when some of them travelled north to Canada. The naval intelligence officer at the yard told Boyer that he was very concerned about reports he had received that the crew were becoming increasingly disaffected.[37] He feared they might try to sabotage *Surcouf* to stop it from going to sea again and in the process damage American ships.

Nevertheless, several of the American dockyard workers made friends with *Surcouf*'s crew. One of these was Robert P Sturtevant, then working as an apprentice in the outside machine shop, who had already been involved in repairs on the British submarines *Pandora*, *Parthian*, and *Truant*.[38] While working in *Surcouf*'s engine room, Sturtevant struck up a friendship with one of the French engineers and, despite language limitations, they got on well together. Sturtevant invited the Frenchman back to his house and took him around in his car.

Some weeks later, just as *Surcouf* was about to sail, the French sailor ran down the gangplank and thrust a package into Sturtevant's hands saying: 'Bob, here's a souvenir. We'll be leaving soon, and we won't be needing it again.' When Sturte-vant opened the package he found a French tricolour from *Surcouf* which now hangs in his house in York, Maine, and is the only surviving flag from the ill-fated submarine. A photograph of this unique flag is included in the picture section.

By September 14 it was clear that repairs would take much longer than the original estimate and the Admiralty advised BAD[*]:

> *Surcouf* – owing to defects found on opening out to be greater than could be anticipated date of completion will not be earlier than end of October.[39]

Earlier, on September 8, Ortoli had received a message from Muselier:

> The continuous development of our naval forces has led me to . . . [create] . . . new staff jobs to be held by officers of outstanding merit. It is therefore my intention to entrust you with important duties at FNFL [Free French naval] headquarters in the near future. Blaison would assume command with Rossignol as his first officer. I fully realize how you will feel at leaving a vessel which you have commissioned and brought to a high standard of fighting efficiency . . . and I know you will respond in the spirit of self-sacrifice.[40]

Reading between the lines it seems likely that it had at last dawned on Muselier – or it was put to him by Horton – that Ortoli was an incompetent captain and that on every occasion he had taken *Surcouf* to sea there had been one or more major disasters. On February 3 1941, Rear Admiral John Godfrey, director of naval intelligence, had circulated a 'Most Secret' report about the Free French navy which included the comment:

> The question of French staff organization is being fought

* The British Admiralty Delegation in Washington.

98

out now and if Admiral Muselier cannot obtain a reasonable decision Admiralty help may be necessary. If Muselier asks for this we can tactfully make certain useful suggestions without hurting anybody's feelings. The Free French navy is operationally part of our own and we are therefore entitled to express our views if, owing to faulty principles of higher command, that force is handicapped, as it is in reaching maximum efficiency. The poor standard . . . is due to the small number of suitable officers Muselier can pick as captains. Senior British officers should send for captains of French ships when dissatisfied with their appearance and discipline and tell them off.[41]

On September 20 Ortoli left and Blaison took command of *Surcouf*. To add to Blaison's worries German intelligence, with the help of the Vichy authorities, had been leaking stories to him that his daughter Francine was in a sanitorium suffering from tuberculosis, and that his wife Thérèse was having an affair with another man. Blaison later explained to a Canadian naval liaison officer, Louis Audette, that this was designed to seduce him away from the Free French and his letters to his wife show the contempt he showed for such rumours.[42] On another occasion, the Germans told Blaison his wife was suffering from advanced cancer.

The senior British officer at Portsmouth was the captain of *Truant*, Lieutenant Commander HAV 'Hughie' Haggard RN, and Boyer discussed with him at length his concern about *Surcouf*, the morale, loyalty of its crew, and its inability to perform any seagoing duty without some major disaster occurring that was endangering everyone on board. As a fellow submariner Haggard readily understood the seriousness of the problem, and was so concerned that he immediately arranged for Boyer to go and see Vice Admiral French, head of the BAD in Washington, and explain the situation to him personally.

A few days later Boyer saw French and told him he was:

Extremely concerned about the state of morale on board

[*Surcouf*] and that I had confirmed evidence from US
Navy intelligence there was a lot of talk around the town
about what they [the crew] were going to do and how
they were not going to take the submarine to sea again.
And there was talk about whether, if they did take the
submarine to sea again, they should try to go back to
Brest and turn their submarine over to the Germans for
which they thought they would get very high praise and
be forgiven for having served with the Free French and
allowed to go back to their families. I also felt the boat
was unsafe and should not be allowed to go to sea again
because the captain and crew were incapable of
operating it satisfactorily.

French heard Boyer out in silence and then, much to Boyer's
amazement, said that in his opinion Boyer's problem was
cowardice, and that he was afraid to take the boat to sea. Boyer
replied:

That as far as being afraid that is undoubtedly true – I
am afraid – and I'd have to be a congenital halfwit not to
be afraid to take such a boat to sea. But this wouldn't
affect me doing my duty as I am called to do it. But I
think it's a bad thing, the boat is valueless to the allied
side, and we're just wasting our time.

Boyer was naturally extremely angry at French's suggestion that
he was a coward but, as a junior officer, could say nothing other
than to ask French if he would make a report to Horton about
what he had said whether he believed him or not. Evidently
French did this because, a few weeks later, Boyer was advised
that a new BNLO was on the way to relieve him.

When Gough and Warner learned that Boyer was leaving the
ship they came to see him separately and begged him to get
them off, too. They told Boyer they hated the ship, had been
very badly treated by the French who were openly hostile
towards them, and regarded them as spies. Boyer was well

aware of all this and, indeed, believed the situation so bad that the three of them had prepared a contingency plan: if the crew mutinied and tried to take the ship back to France, the liaison team would barricade themselves in the radio room with drawn guns, destroy the cipher books and send a distress signal. Boyer told Gough and Warner he would do everything he could to get them transferred, and went to see Haggard again to ask for his help.

Two days before he was to leave *Surcouf*, Boyer had a farewell meeting with Blaison who handed him a letter thanking him for his work and loyal service to the Free French cause.[43] It was a very nice gesture and, since a copy went to Horton, helped redress the allegations of cowardice made by French. Even so, Boyer did not like to tell Blaison that throughout his time in *Surcouf* his incompetence, and the near total disasters on each occasion they had gone to sea, had had him in a state of almost perpetual fear of what stupidity Blaison and his crew would commit next.

On November 5 1941, the new BNLO arrived and Gough and Warner said an emotional goodbye to Boyer as he left *Surcouf*. On the jetty Boyer turned and waved to them. Somehow he knew he would never see them again. Fifty years later their memory is still very strong and Boyer admits:

I'm prejudiced with regard to Warner and Gough. I felt they were both exceptional men and they gave me loyalty and assistance far beyond anything I could have expected. I did my best to get them taken off. Even now when I don't sleep they are often with me.[44]

NOTES

1. Report No. 829/0080 by Captain Read, April 15 1941, ADM 199/1144 (PRO, Kew).
2. *The War At Sea*, Captain SW Roskill DSC RN (HMSO, 1954), vol 1, 375.
3. *Who Killed Surcouf?*, George Young (privately published, Canada, 1986), 28.

4. Message No. 12, April 8 1941 (Vincennes Archives, Paris).

5. A 10,549-ton merchant ship built in 1926 and converted to an armed merchant cruiser in October 1939, the *Salopian* was sunk by a U-boat in the Atlantic on May 13 1941.

6. A 5583-ton steamer, *Nerissa* was sunk by a U-boat on April 30 1941.

7. ADM 199/1144 (PRO, Kew).

8. *Surcouf* report, April 1–17, No. 773/SM 4164, May 3 1941, ADM 199/1120 (PRO, Kew)

9. *Surcouf* report ADM 199/1858, Folio 650 (PRO, Kew).

10. ADM 199/1120, (PRO, Kew).

11. *Leakage of information re French submarine Surcouf*, letter No. 06967/41 of June 10 1941 and letter NS 1023-8-15 from Rear Admiral Nelles, both ADM 199/1120 (PRO, Kew).

12. Ortoli letter *op. cit.*

13. Letter No. SM/117, May 3 1941 (Vincennes Archives, Paris).

14. Ortoli letter, *op.cit.*

15. Boyer interview, Dublin, June 1990.

16. *Ibid*.

17. Originally the two-man crew for *Surcouf*'s aircraft had come from the French navy's own air service, the *Aéronavale*, but evidently they refused to serve under de Gaulle after the takeover and were repatriated to France. They were replaced by two members of the French air force thus explaining their non-maritime rank. Sadly, Sergeant Hazard was killed on June 21 1942 while serving with the RAAF, and his name is listed amongst the *Forces Aériennes Françaises Libres* (FAFL). Information kindly supplied by Mr F Neave, Northwood, NSW, Australia, letter January 5 1987 to RN Submarine Museum, and M. Gilbert Bloch. Several accounts of *Surcouf* after mid 1941 mention her carrying an aircraft but this could not have been possible.

18. Interview with Mme Thérèse Blaison, Paris, June 1990. The author is greatly indebted to Mme Blaison for making available her late husband's letters for use in this book.

19. Mlle Francine Blaison died in 1988.

20. Message No. 300, April 24 1941 (Vincennes Archives, Paris).

21. Message No. 435, May 15 1941 (Vincennes Archives, Paris).

22. Folio 7396 (Vincennes Archives, Paris).

23. Letter SO/E7, May 14 1941, ADM 199/1858, Folio 656, (PRO, Kew).

24. Boyer interview.

25. The airfield is still there to this day, and the US Navy make part of it available, at their expense, as Bermuda's international airport.

26. Often incorrectly claimed to be the codename for Sir William

Stephenson himself.

27. The author is most grateful to Herbert Tatum, Whitey Froud, and many other Bermudians who telephoned after his programme on VSB Radio giving details of the location of 'Benker', and Mr and Mrs Baker. Some years later the Bakers left 'Benker' but took the name with them. The house is now owned by Mr Peter Chapman who very kindly gave the author permission to enter the grounds and photograph it.

28. Message No. 1062, July 3 1941 (Vincennes Archives, Paris).

29. OP-23G, Serial 213923, Record Group 181, Box 43, File EF13/L9-3 (161) (National Archives, Mass, USA).

30. ADM 199/1858 (PRO, Kew).

31. A submarine's buoyancy is controlled by ballast tanks that can be filled with water or air. In simple non-technical terms, each tank is fitted with two sets of valves. At the bottom is the kingston valve that admits water. At the top are the air vents. If the two sets of valves are open together the ballast tank will fill with water and the submarine will dive. If the air vents are closed and high-pressure air is blown into the tank, the water will be forced out through the kingston valve and the submarine rises.

32. ADM 199/1858 (PRO, Kew).

33. Project Order L1/DA (27) (278) (National Archives, Mass, USA).

34. Letter from CA Griffiths, Bureau of Ships, Navy Department, Washington, DC, August 6 1941, EF13/L9, Project 161 (National Archives, Mass, USA).

35. Boyer interview.

36. Letter to author, December 8 1990.

37. Boyer interview.

38. Letter from Mr Robert P Sturtevant to the author, October 16 1990.

39. Message No. 2107, September 14 1941, (Vincennes Archives, Paris).

40. Message No. 1659, September 8 1941, (Vincennes Archives, Paris).

41. NID 0651, February 3 1941, FO 371/28452 (PRO, Kew).

42. Letter from Mr Louis C Audette OC QC, Ottawa, July 25 1990.

43. Boyer interview.

44. *Surcouf – Diving to Disaster*, Television South West, September 8 1987, a copy of the master tape very kindly made available to the author by the producer Frank Wintle.

CHAPTER 6

CANADIAN INTRIGUE

The new BNLO for *Surcouf* was Roger John Gilbert Burney[1] who was born on March 25 1919 at Fleet in Hampshire, the youngest of three children. His brother Christopher[2] was two years older, born in June 1917, and his sister Joan, the oldest, born in December 1914. Roger's father, Lieutenant Colonel Arthur Edward Cave Arthur 'Jack' Burney, was a regular army officer serving in the Royal Artillery, and had been awarded the Military Cross and Distinguished Service Order during the landings at Gallipoli in World War I.

When Roger was aged two the entire family went out to India as his father had been posted to the North-West frontier where the Burneys stayed until 1926 when, on their return to England, they went to live in Hertfordshire. Soon afterwards Colonel Burney was sent back to India again with only his wife Dorothy accompanying him, leaving the three children to be sent off to school by their grandparents. Roger's first school was Heddon Court, a large country house at Cockfosters in north-east London set in what was then open country, and later he went to Bilton Grange, near Rugby.

Unfortunately, during his second tour of duty in India, Roger's father contracted pneumonia which affected his heart and he was invalided home and posted to the Royal School of Artillery at Larkhill. Sadly he was never to fully recover his health and, in 1931 when Roger was only twelve, he died suddenly at the supper table in front of the entire family.

Since they were living in military quarters Colonel Burney's sudden death not only meant that his wife had to find alternative accommodation within a month, but also left her in considerable financial difficulty since at first her pension was only £80 a year, although, because her husband had contracted his illness while on active service, this was later increased to £120 per year.[3] As a result plans that Christopher and Roger would go to Stowe College had to be abandoned. Fortunately Wellington College gave both of them an exhibition (subsequently converted to a foundation),[4] a form of scholarship for sons of army officers who had financial problems.

Roger went to Wellington College from 1932 until 1937 during which time he became head of his house. In December 1936 he won a Kitchener Scholarship to Peterhouse College, Cambridge, arriving there in October 1937 to study French history.[5]

In 1938 Burney met the twenty-eight-year-old tenor Peter Pears[6] who lived near Cambridge. Pears came from a strong Quaker family and was an ardent pacifist. Evidently he took a great liking to Burney, and a close homosexual relationship soon developed between them. Burney often stayed with Pears in his London apartment at 67, Hallam Street. Burney obviously enjoyed these visits and on one occasion wrote from his family house at Hay in Herefordshire, thanking Pears:

> It is difficult to say this satisfactorily but I think you do know how much I enjoyed it and how remarkably it has affected me. Oh dear – oh dear – it's all so illogical. The more I live the more I feel immature, and the more I want to live. I find myself now with three main things I'm interested in – music, painting, and writing. Only my own intimate knowledge of my own inadequacy stops me setting out on your kind of road . . . so I must do what I can with my violin . . . I understand so little about the theory of music . . . can you help me?

Burney also met Pears' lover, the twenty-five-year-old composer

Benjamin Britten,[7] and the friendship between the three became very close causing Burney to write to Pears:

> I know quite well how busy he [Britten] is. I only write now to stake an early claim on him and, if you will be there too, then on you too.

The influence of Pears and Britten caused Burney to become a pacifist and, at the outbreak of war in September 1939, he went before a tribunal where his views were recognized and he was exempted from military service. He then applied to join the Quaker Ambulance Service. Meanwhile, Pears and Britten had left Britain for America in mid 1939 where they remained until 1942.

However, the sinking of the unarmed passenger liner *Athenia*[8] by the Germans during the first days of the war changed Burney's views and, at the end of the summer term in 1940, he left Cambridge and joined the Royal Naval Volunteer Reserve (RNVR) as a rating. After training at Portsmouth, Burney was posted to HMS *Birmingham* for a few months and was then selected for officer training at HMS *King Alfred*, the shore establishment at Brighton, from which he emerged after three months a very raw and inexperienced sublieutenant.

Burney then volunteered for submarines and did a short course at HMS *Dolphin* at Gosport after which, on September 3 1941, he was sent to HMS *Elfin*, a shore establishment at Blyth in Northumberland, for training in liaison duties. In keeping with the traditions of the armed services because Burney was fluent in French the Navy posted him to a Dutch submarine. However, Boyer's sudden unpopularity with Admiral French resulted in Burney's posting being changed to *Surcouf*, and in October 1941 he sailed for America.

On arrival Burney took some leave and went and stayed with Pears and Britten who were then living with Mrs Elizabeth Mayer at her house at Amityville, Long Island. On November 5 he travelled to Portsmouth, New Hampshire, to join *Surcouf* which was still under repair but, unlike Greene and Boyer, Burney had not been warned by Horton as to what he might expect.

Burney was a dedicated Francophile. He had studied French history at Cambridge, believed de Gaulle was the saviour of France, and that *Surcouf* represented the best of submarine technology. For Boyer it was terribly sad. Here was this highly intelligent, sensitive young man, so keen to do well, fired with enthusiasm for the French, fresh from training with no submarine experience, and yet unwilling to listen to any of Boyer's cautionary advice. Indeed, Burney told Boyer that his dislike of *Surcouf* was simply because he (Boyer) could not understand the French mentality which had soured his appreciation of their motivation and achievements.

After a day with Burney handing over the confidential books, Boyer could do no more. Burney believed Boyer was an Anglophile, tired and cynical. Perhaps he was. Boyer wished him luck and went off to Halifax. After a few weeks' delay he was allocated passage back to Britain in the 800-ton submarine *Jastrzab* (the ex-HMS *P-551* on loan to the Polish navy) enduring a particularly long and stormy voyage.

Repairs to *Surcouf* continued through September and October as more defects came to light. In early September Blaison had unexpectedly asked that all the main engine bearings in the two Sulzer diesels should be remetalled, but this was such a large task that a meeting was held on September 15 with Blaison at which Captain HFD Davis USN, of the navy yard, explained:

> The condition of the ship [*Surcouf*] was much worse than was appreciated [originally] and that in practically every case where a part of the ship was opened up it was found that [additional] work would be necessary . . . this introduced doubt in the minds of the yard whether the ship would be in a satisfactory condition on completion of the overhaul unless additional work was undertaken. The present completion date was October 4 but if new main bearings were to be fitted then this would be extended to at least October 22 [and] . . . new [US Navy submarine] construction was being delayed by the

107

[*Surcouf*'s] overhaul.[9]

On October 29, much to the relief of the Americans, *Surcouf* left the dry dock she had been occupying for three months. There were still many small defects[10] to complete and it was not until November 10 that Blaison signed the receipt[11] for his ship having been repaired to his satisfaction. He then re-embarked its ammunition including 300 rounds of 8-inch shells, 288 cases of 37mm cartridges, fourteen 21.5-inch and seven 16-inch torpedoes. On November 11, *Surcouf* sailed from Portsmouth under its own power down the coast, past Nantucket, to the main US Navy submarine base at Groton, New London, Massachusetts. Situated at the entrance to Long Island Sound where there was deep water, sea trials were carried out with an American submarine so as to test all *Surcouf*'s systems.

Before leaving Portsmouth, Blaison gave an interview to *Time* magazine which, in its issue for November 10 1941, reported:

Convalescent Weapon

The heaviest submarine in the world is ready to go back into action. Captain Louis Blaison told his countrymen by short-wave radio last week that his vessel would soon again 'seek out the enemy'. His vessel is the huge *Surcouf* which has been in Portsmouth, NH, for repairs . . . she is so big that she carries a seaplane in a hangar aft of her turret. Most of *Surcouf*'s crew left her . . . when France fell, and chose to return home. Captain Blaison told how he got her back in service: 'With a small nucleus of veteran submarine men we built up a crew. We transformed fishermen into gunners, peasants and college boys into electricians, and firemen and soldiers into mechanics.'[12]

Although this may have looked good in print, the real truth was that Blaison was still desperately short of trained crew. On November 15, he cabled Muselier telling him that one of his engineers, George Martin, would be in the local US Navy hospital for a month, and one of his best electricians, Jean Thomas, was also unfit for duty.[13] The level of ill health amongst *Surcouf*'s crew was always particularly high – far higher than British submarines – and much of this may have been deliberately exaggerated as an excuse to get off the vessel. During the repairs a group of navy-yard workers complained of soreness to their eyes which was later diagnosed as conjunctivitis resulting from the acid spilt from the batteries which had corroded the metalwork in the bilges.

Blaison sent a second message to Muselier:

> Informing you of my urgent needs in personnel. Three electricians, quartermasters or sailors. Eight mechanics . . . [and] one torpedo petty officer.[14]

It does not seem that Muselier sent any reply or was able to do anything to help Blaison. A week earlier on November 8, the Foreign Office had sent a message to its diplomatic missions in Iceland, New York, Mexico City, Montevideo, Buenos Aires, Cairo, and Lisbon:

> From General de Gaulle, No. 2468.
> Free French navy is especially interested in French volunteers . . . minimum age seventeen good education knowledge of English for following specialities: radio, signalman, asdic, engineer, air pilots, electricians.[15]

Surcouf began its sea trials at New London on November 21 giving Burney his first opportunity of seeing the submarine in action. He was not to be disappointed. The following day *Surcouf* collided with the American submarine with which it was exercising resulting in leaks in numbers 3 and 4 of *Surcouf*'s forward ballast tanks.

The damage was sufficiently severe for *Surcouf* to have gone back to Portsmouth and into dry dock for proper inspection and repairs but, apart from the fact that the dock now had an

American submarine in it, Blaison realized he had already out-stayed his welcome. He decided it was not serious enough to stop him from sailing. Finally, on November 27 1941, *Surcouf* left New London for Bermuda where she arrived three days later and once more came under the command of Kennedy-Purvis at HMS *Malabar*.

Surcouf's orders were unchanged and the Admiralty expected her to recommence operations in the South Atlantic searching for German surface raiders. There was even a suggestion that she might go on into the Indian Ocean, where German raiders had been particularly active, and end up at Singapore or Australia. *Surcouf* could refuel at Gibraltar and Cape Town. The Greek steamer *Marika Protopapa* was loaded in Bermuda with spares for *Surcouf*, including some 8-inch shells and torpedoes, and sailed for Cape Town where there was a large Royal Naval base, since none of the Royal Navy depots around the world carried sizes to fit *Surcouf*.

However, instead of sailing direct for the South Atlantic, *Surcouf* left Bermuda on December 7 for Halifax, Nova Scotia, because Blaison told *Malabar* that Muselier, who was arriving there on December 12 with the three corvettes *Mimosa*, *Alysse* and *Aconit*, wanted to inspect all the units of the Free French navy operating in that area. It was during this voyage from Bermuda to Halifax that another event occurred which later fuelled more rumours about *Surcouf*.

On December 8, about 550 miles south of Halifax, the Norwegian tanker *Atlantic* reported that at 10 am that day she was:

Chased by large submarine wearing a French flag. We had to steer all points of the compass to avoid her. She then disappeared in a NNW direction.[16]

The *Atlantic* broadcast a distress call that she was under attack and inevitably the incident generated claims that *Surcouf* was trying to sink her, but the facts do not bear this out even if she had been capable of firing her torpedoes at anyone.

After *Surcouf* arrived at Halifax on December 10, Burney

110

wrote his first report to Horton.[17] The first month on board had obviously had a salutary effect on Burney and his enthusiasm for the French had quickly evaporated.

During the time he had been in Bermuda Burney was delighted to find an old school friend from Wellington, Frank Giles, who was ADC to the governor, Lord Knollys. Giles invited Burney to stay in Government House and did all he could to cheer up his lonely and bewildered friend suddenly caught in the crossfire of divided French loyalties. Burney later wrote to Giles from Halifax:

> I have been experiencing a reign of terror ever since I left you, and not a soul to talk to, nothing to do but mope in my loneliness . . . I am afraid you did me no good at all because I feel this loneliness far more keenly now. I could write of the many amusing and horrifying incidents that have already occurred since I left [Bermuda].[18]

While in Halifax, Burney was able to take a few days' leave staying with the Mayers, Pears, and Britten at Amityville and, on December 18, he wrote from Halifax thanking Mrs Mayer:

> Please forgive my inglorious silence after such hospitality . . . I hope you will put it down to the many preoccupations that have hedged me in since I saw you . . . how exhausting it has been. Sometimes I feel as if I had sold my soul in this job. You know how uninteresting the French bourgeoisie can be. They are my only companions – talking about their wenches and especially about certain places in port they know all day, and affording me the least companionship possible. In fact I don't think I have ever felt so lonely. I had a brief respite in Bermuda with the most charming people on the island – but all that and Amityville included – only throws the poverty of one's present situation into greater relief. Your hospitality makes me long to return and

indeed I hope my luck will not be so bad as to keep me away for too long. I feel terribly homesick for America and I miss being amongst people who are physically pleasing, too! I'm writing to Peter [Pears] separately. I wish I could write you more coherently and exactly.[19]

Burney's sudden and unpleasant conversion from Francophile to Francophobe was reflected in his extremely thoughtful reports, the first of which explained that while in America during the three-month refit the crew, who had little to do, had been greatly influenced by direct information from Vichy France. Unlike in Britain, information was freely available because America had diplomatic relations with the Vichy government. Quite a number of the crew had also gone on leave to Canada where, in the Quebec area, Pétain was very popular. As a result Burney concluded:

> They frequently question amongst themselves the services being rendered by the Free French forces and especially in its operations against the French themselves. Generally their analysis is not so clear . . . but because the issues are not clear the majority are open to any strong influences . . . and the majority of influences are against the Free French movement. The lack of a firm and respected captain makes any dangers that may arise on this account, far more serious.

Burney then dealt with the question of leadership and said the men frequently refused to carry out orders; they simply walked away from the officer giving them. Having served as a rating on board Royal Navy warships before becoming an officer, this came as a great shock to Burney who also commented that there was:

> Great hostility between the petty officers and the men, but I have had no experiences with which I can compare these, and this may be quite normal in French warships.

112

Burney's main criticism was reserved for Blaison who had a disconcerting habit of asking him for advice on operational matters which Burney was not in a position to give. Explaining the incident with the tanker *Atlantic* Burney wrote:

> The captain asked me to tell him: the procedure for stopping and questioning a merchant ship; whether we should stop her or not; whether we should continue trying to identify her; whether we should disclose our own identity; whether we should hoist a large ensign [flag]; and whether we should alter course as the result of the distress signal made by the *Atlantic*, and if so, which way. During the incident *Surcouf* never once tried to get into a suitable position for attack or defence; during the most critical part of the investigation she was beam on to the stern of the tanker whose gun . . . was trained on us; none of our guns was manned. These facts can be corroborated by a Canadian naval officer who was taking passage with us to Halifax and was on the bridge at the time.

Far from *Surcouf* chasing the *Atlantic* and trying to sink her, Blaison and a young inexperienced British officer, who had never been to sea in a submarine before, were having an animated debate on the bridge as to what they should do. Apart from demolishing another *Surcouf* rumour, the incident shows the bizarre state of affairs existing in *Surcouf* and how she was far more of a danger to herself than any other ship.

Surcouf's voyage to Halifax had nothing to do with a review of naval forces by Muselier, but was a deliberate deceit to conceal an operation that he and de Gaulle had planned in order to further their authority. Ever since he arrived in London de Gaulle had encountered great problems in commanding the allegiance of the French empire. Indo-China, the Middle East, and North Africa had all declared their loyalty to Vichy; so, too, had the important island of Martinique in the West Indies. De Gaulle therefore decided that he must show that he commanded

French affairs anywhere in the world.

As a result, he turned his attention to the small group of islands about twelve miles off the south coast of Newfoundland called St Pierre and Miquelon, which were governed by Gilbert de Bournat, a Vichy sympathizer.[20] The islands had some strategic importance because they lay off the mouth of the St Lawrence river where convoys for Britain assembled. On St Pierre there was a powerful radio transmitter which, because of the anti-British sentiments of the local government, it was believed was sending back to the Vichy government in France details of convoy movements that were subsequently passed on to the Germans.

After Pétain had assumed office following the armistice in June 1940 Newfoundland asked London for permission to take over these islands with Canada's help, if necessary, since at the time Newfoundland was not part of Canada but a British crown colony. The Foreign Office was not enthusiastic and explained that the integrity of France's North American possessions was assured by the Monroe Doctrine but, nevertheless, asked Newfoundland to work out what forces might be required for such an operation.

Churchill was well aware of the situation but had to tread warily. America had diplomatic relations with the Vichy government and disliked de Gaulle. At this critical moment of the war when American aid was essential to Britain's survival and the Japanese menace in the Far East was growing stronger daily, Churchill had no intention of upsetting Roosevelt. Naturally, de Gaulle saw things rather differently:

It was . . . scandalous that, quite close to Newfoundland, a small French archipelago, whose population was asking to join us, should be kept in obedience to Vichy. The British, haunted by the idea that . . . German submarines might . . . receive assistance [from] the radio station on St Pierre, wished it to be rallied. But according to them, Washington's agreement was necessary. I considered this agreement desirable, but not indispensable since this was

114

Top right: Charles Qualls Peters, left), who first heard of the bombing of the *Surcouf* by the US ir force in February 1942. Next to im is Freddy, a local Cuna Indian, hen John Mann, and far right, Ricardo. In the centre is the donkey riginally bought by John Mann for 3. The photograph was taken in 955 at San Blas point. *John Mann)*

Middle right: Group of officers on oard *Surcouf* in autumn 1941. rom left: Frances Boyer, Louis Blaison (captain), George Russignol, Andre Leoquet gunnery officer), and Pierre Le Grand (second engineer). On the ulkhead behind Louis Blaison is a icture of Robert Surcouf in action gainst the British. The picture ives some idea of the enormous ize of *Surcouf's* internal layout ompared to a conventional ubmarine of the time. *Francis Boyer)*

elow right: Two members of the ritish naval liaison team. Left: eading Signalman Harold Varner, right, Leading elegraphist Bernard Gough. The hotograph was taken in January 942 in the Hotel Robert, at St ierre. *(Stanley Warner)*

elow left: Sub Lt Roger Burney NVR, who served as liaison fficer in *Surcouf* from November 941 until her loss in February 1942. pre-war friend of Benjamin ritten, the composer dedicated his *ar Requiem* to Roger Burney. *Irs Joan Adams)*

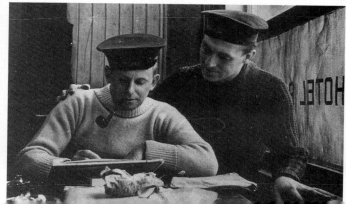

Left: Henri Le Bousse being visited in Camp Hill Hospital, Halifax, Nova Scotia, in March 1941, by some of his colleagues from *Surcouf*. On the left is chief engineer George Dupuy, in the middle an unidentified Canadian officer, on the right second engineer Pierre Le Grand. Dupuy left *Surcouf* in January 1942 and took charge of the defences of St Pierre & Miquelon *(Le Bousse)*

Below left: Henri Le Bousse with Miss Ruth Smith (now Mrs MacDonald) in Camp Hill Hospital, Halifax, Nova Scotia in March 1941, after injuring his left hand on board *Surcouf*. *(Mrs E. MacDonald)*

Below right: Mrs MacDonald at her house in Nova Scotia in November 1990, reading the letter from Henri Le Bousse who Mrs MacDonald had nursed in 1941, and thought had died in *Surcouf*.

French submarine *Surcouf* at Halifax, Nova Scotia in 1941. *(Maritime Museum of the Atlantic, Halifax.)*

Surcouf undergoing repairs in Nbr.2 dry-dock at the US Navy yard at Portsmouth, New Hampshire in September 1941. *(US Navy archives, Portsmouth)*

One of the 3,800hp Sulzer diesel motors fitted to *Surcouf*. *(National Archives, Washington DC)*

View of *Surcouf*'s main engine room. *(ECPA, Paris, #218)*

Below left: The aircraft hangar on *Surcouf*, just behind the conning tower, which housed a small seaplane. Immediately above the hangar are two Hotchkiss 37mm canons. *(National Archives, Washington DC)*

Below right: The twin 203mm guns on *Surcouf*. *(National Archives, Washington DC)*

General De Gaulle leaving *Surcouf* after an inspection of the submarine at Devonport. *(Imperial War Museum)*

Below left: Captain Louis Blaison (far right) who served in *Surcouf* throughout her service with the Free French Navy, and was in command from September 1941 until her disappearance in February 1942, talking with officers from the French frigate *Mimosa* at St Pierre in December 1941. *(ECPA, Paris #228)*

Above right: Admiral Émile Muselier inspecting the crew of *Surcouf*, either at St Pierre or Halifax in December 1941. On Muselier's right is Louis Blaison. *(ECPA, Paris #343)*

Right: Captain Louis Blaison and some of his crew on the bridge of the *Surcouf* at St Pierre in December 1941. Immediately in front of Captain Blaison is the identification flare which was fired when challenged by another allied ship or aircraft. *(ECPA, Paris #700)*

Above: Damage to the American freighter *Thompson Lykes* after colliding with an unidentified vessel off Panama on 18 February 1942. The photograph was taken in dry-dock in New Orleans.
(National Archives, Washington DC)

Above: Tricolour from *Surcouf* given to Mr Sturtevant at the end of her refit at the Portsmouth navy yard in 1941. It is the only tricolour belonging to *Surcouf* in existence. *(Robert Sturtevant)*

Below: Colonel Harold Staley USAAF (cen[ ] back row) with his crew and his B-17 Flying Fortress *Black Jack*. *(Harold Staley)*

ew of *Surcouf* while undergoing training at Holy Loch, in Scotland in late 1940.
nperial War Museum)

rcouf under repair at Portsmouth Navy Yard in late 1941. On the right is HMS *Pandora* also under
pair. *(Norman Holt)*

Aerial view of *Guaca* cemetery at San Blas, Panama. Bodies of sailors washed-up in the area in February 1942 were brought to the cemetery by local Cuna Indians and buried in the white area in the centre.

John Mann, a Cuna Indian expert, standing in the *Guaca*, or foreigners cemetery, at San Blas. The graves have fallen in and are largely overgrown.

merely an internal French affair [emphasis added].[21]

Internal French matter St Pierre and Miquelon was most certainly not and no one knew this better than de Gaulle. On October 13 1941, de Gaulle wrote to Anthony Eden, the Foreign Secretary, recommending that he should seize the islands using ships of his Free French navy. A week later Eden replied that he would have to consult the Canadian and American governments because of their geographical position.

In view of the Far East situation it was hardly surprising that the Foreign Office, and the State Department in Washington, had other things to occupy them with the result that nothing happened. On December 9 (the day after war with Japan had commenced), Muselier, by then in Newfoundland, cabled de Gaulle in London that he was ready to seize St Pierre and Miquelon. The signal was naturally read by the Government Code and Cipher School (GCCS), Britain's codebreaking centre at Bletchley Park near London,[22] and passed to Major Desmond Morton[23] who was responsible for Churchill seeing all important intelligence it derived, including the German Ultra decrypts.

It says much for Churchill's abilities that, at a time when he was dealing with defeat in North Africa, attacks on Hong Kong and Malaya, and the loss of HMS *Prince of Wales* and HMS *Repulse*, he had time to spare to bother about two small islands. Nevertheless, Churchill thought it would be a good idea to keep de Gaulle occupied – and happy – by letting him seize the islands in the name of the Free French.

On December 13 Churchill told his chief of staff, General Sir Hastings Ismay:

I am hoping to make an offer . . . [about the islands] . . .
to Pétain in the names of Great Britain and USA. I do
not think this prospect would be marred by a Free
French descent upon Miquelon and St Pierre; it would be
more convenient *after* [original emphasis] an Anglo–
American ultimatum has been delivered and rejected,
but if you feel it is better to unmuzzle Muselier now I am

prepared to consent.[24]

Ismay then cabled Lord Halifax, the British ambassador in Washington, that Free French headquarters in London were being told that Britain saw no objection to their plan but that de Gaulle had been asked to wait for thirty-six hours so that the American government could be told. Although still reeling from the Pearl Harbor attack, Roosevelt told Halifax the next day that he was most strongly opposed to any Free French action against the islands.

At 10.50 am the following morning, December 17, François Dejean from de Gaulle's office went to the Foreign Office where he saw William Strang, an assistant under-secretary. He was told of Roosevelt's views and that, accordingly, no action must be taken by the Free French; it was vital that if any orders had been issued by Muselier that they should at once be cancelled. Strang added that the Canadian and American governments were discussing a plan by which they would send civilian personnel to take over control of the radio station.

Dejean was asked to confirm that any orders relating to the proposed Free French seizure had been cancelled and, later that morning, he telephoned the Foreign Office confirming this. To make quite sure Strang sent Dejean a letter that same day saying:

> In view of this message [from Roosevelt] we had no alternative but to ask General de Gaulle not to proceed further with the proposed operation . . . you were good enough to tell me later in the morning that no orders for the operation had in fact been issued and that it would not be carried out by Free French naval forces.[25]

Satisfied that there could be no misunderstanding the Foreign Office then cabled this information to Halifax who in turn passed it on to the President.

At the time all this was happening Churchill was on his way to America having sailed from Gourock, on the Clyde in Scotland,

116

on December 13 in the battleship HMS *Duke of York*, sister ship to the *Prince of Wales* sunk only three days earlier by the Japanese off Malaya. The Foreign Secretary, Anthony Eden, was also absent, visiting Russia. Under these circumstances the St Pierre and Miquelon affair enjoyed a low priority.

In the meantime Muselier's little armada of *Surcouf* and the three corvettes sat waiting in Halifax. The Canadian director of naval operations in Halifax at HMCS *Stadacona* was Commander HG De Wolff RCN, and Muselier assured him that he only wanted to take the four ships to sea to see how well they operated together.[26] Meanwhile, Blaison had told Burney that they were going to occupy St Pierre and Miquelon and that Muselier was going to Washington and Ottawa to get their approval for the operation.[27] Burney had been told nothing by the Admiralty nor by Muselier when he arrived back at Halifax on December 19 having failed to get approval for the operation from either government.

The following morning, December 20, at 10.15 am Burney overheard *Surcouf*'s chief engineer, George Dupuis, mention they were to sail at 11 am with the three corvettes and carry out some exercises at sea. Burney went to the control room to find out details of the exercise programme but could get no information. At 11.55 am the four ships sailed and only then did Blaison tell him that after the exercises the ships would proceed straight to St John's, Newfoundland.

For the next three days the four ships carried out exercises which even to Burney's inexperienced eye seemed to have little purpose. The weather was appalling and as usual *Surcouf* rolled so badly – reaching 40° – that acid spilled from the new batteries starting electrical fires as had happened on previous voyages. Burney realized something odd was happening when *Surcouf* altered course as a result of orders passed by line-throwing guns from one of the corvettes (to avoid using radio).[28] When Burney tried to find out what was happening, no one including Blaison would tell him anything.

At 7.30 am on the morning of December 24 Burney awoke to find himself off St Pierre and, although *Surcouf* was too large to enter the harbour, her landing party of twenty sailors joined those from the corvettes and soon rounded up the pro-Vichy supporters who were put in the local prison. The radio station was occupied and by 8 am the Free French flag flew over the port and de Gaulle had his victory.

The first the British government knew about any of this was on Christmas Day when the Admiralty received a cable from Muselier saying:

> I have the honour to inform you that in compliance with orders quite recently received from General de Gaulle and at the request of inhabitants I have proceeded this morning to island St Pierre and rallied people to Free France and allied cause with enthusiastic reception.[29]

The Admiralty told the Foreign Office who asked them to repeat the message to the British Admiralty Delegation in Washington for Churchill and Lord Halifax with the added note that 'this action has come as a complete surprise to us'. Dejean was immediately sent for by the Foreign Office and explained with obvious embarrassment that he had been told nothing of the operation. The next day de Gaulle was summoned and gave a very tortuous explanation of events which was later described in the Foreign Office report as 'dishonest'.

The news broke like a bombshell over the *Arcadia* conference in Washington where Churchill was trying to persuade Roosevelt to finish Hitler off first before attacking Japan. It was particularly embarrassing for Churchill, who had originally approved the operation in order to placate de Gaulle, and now had to apologize to Roosevelt for de Gaulle's deliberate deceit.

Like Churchill, Roosevelt also had far more important things to worry about and was ready to shrug off the affair which he described as a 'teapot tempest'.[30] Secretary of State Cordell Hull, however, a career diplomat of the old school, was infuriated by de Gaulle's duplicity and assured the Pétain government in Vichy that America did not recognize the takeover which he described in a statement as:

The action taken by the three so-called Free French ships at Saint Pierre-Miquelon was an arbitary action contrary to the agreement of all parties and certainly without the prior knowledge or consent of the United States government.

Hull became so incensed, even threatening to resign, that he tried to get the Canadians to send a force to the islands and oust de Gaulle's forces. Unfortunately this plan backfired because Ottawa told him they were delighted with the takeover and had no intention of interfering. Hull retreated deeply offended and nurtured a hatred against de Gaulle for the rest of the war.

De Gaulle took issue with Hull's expression 'so-called' and a long exchange of diplomatic telegrams followed until a form of words could be found that suited all parties. In the end the affair was submerged by world events. As America had been brought into the war in such a cataclysmic manner Churchill no longer felt it necessary to behave so cautiously towards them as he had done when America was neutral. In any case he was pleased that the islands were no longer under Vichy control and that de Gaulle had had his moment of triumph as this would help to establish his leadership in other French colonies. At a time when there was little good news the newsreels exploited the seizure as a great victory and a British war correspondent, Bishop Marshall, took some heroic photographs of the victorious invasion.

During the nights of December 27 and 28, *Surcouf* patrolled the entrance to the harbour of St Pierre since Muselier believed Vichy warships might try an attack. Blaison told Burney that he thought American warships might also try and intervene. When Burney asked Blaison what his orders were he replied that Muselier had told him to fire on any ships other than British, adding: 'And if they are American it's just too bad'. As nothing happened the excitement soon palled and by December 31 the crew of *Surcouf* had turned to other interests as Burney's report to Horton of January 1 records:

Last night almost everyone on board was drunk and had

119

the enemy chosen to attack then we would certainly have been captured intact without the least difficulty. I have said to Muselier and Blaison that I am attached to *Surcouf* to help her in her operations, particularly by maintaining communication with the Admiralty . . . and that I must be kept informed of all plans . . . throughout the whole operation the Free French naval authorities have given [me] the least possible help and confidence. So far as I know we have not received any direct Admiralty approval for the operation.[31]

Burney's report reached Horton (but like all the other BNLO reports was not shown to the French) around the time Boyer finally got back to Britain. As a result when he went to see Horton instead of being unpopular because of Admiral French's allegations of cowardice, Boyer found himself:

High man on the totem pole. I was terribly popular and got two glasses of sherry because everything I had said had come true, and Horton knew I'd said it. Horton asked me how things had been on board and I told him they were terrible – in fact I told him exactly what I'd told French.[32]

Apart from the fact that Boyer's comments matched those of Burney by this time de Gaulle and Muselier were highly unpopular with Churchill. Thus Horton was able to ignore the previous political considerations that had obliged him to keep *Surcouf* in service against his will. It is clear that Horton had deliberately downgraded the role of BNLO in *Surcouf*. First he had chosen Greene, a brilliant submariner, only to have him insulted by Ortoli; next Boyer, also very experienced who had proved himself in another French submarine, only to be accused of cowardice when he told Admiral French the truth; so now Horton decided not to waste any more experienced officers on this useless ship which was why he had sent Burney to this unpopular post.

Boyer certainly had a charmed life. The *Sfax* in which he served in 1940 was torpedoed by the *U-37* in December 1940; the *Jastrzab* was accidentally sunk off Norway on May 2 1942 by the destroyer HMS *St Albans*[33] and the minesweeper HMS *Seagull*; and *Surcouf* was lost with all hands four months after he left. After serving in HMS *L-27*[34] and the American Lend-Lease submarine *P-554*, in 1943 Boyer went back into general service and became the Royal Navy's youngest destroyer captain in command of HMS *Roxborough* which had begun life as the USS *Foote*, and was one of the fifty destroyers given to Britain in 1940 in exchange for America acquiring a number of bases on British territory. In March 1943 when returning from America, Boyer was allocated space in HMS *Harvester* but half an hour before she sailed from Halifax (with all his gear already on board) his space was commandeered by a senior officer. Boyer took passage in HMS *Escapade* with the same convoy, sleeping on the wardroom sofa; three days out of Halifax, on March 11, *Harvester* was sunk with all her crew.

On January 7 1942, while *Surcouf* was still in St Pierre, the two replacements for Gough and Warner that Boyer had asked Haggard to arrange arrived.[35] They were Leading Telegraphist John Green and Signalman Lawrence Stannard both of whom had been serving in the submarine HMS *L-27* which was doing Asdic trials off Harbor Place, Newfoundland. Green was aged twenty-eight and had joined submarines in July 1938; he had already served with the Free French submarine *Rubis* in 1940. Stannard was only twenty and had joined submarines the year before in June 1941.

They found *Surcouf* covered in ice with huge icicles hanging from the two guns. Gough and Warner took them below and handed over the confidential books and explained their duties. Both Stannard and Green were appalled by what they found and made no secret of the fact that they disliked their new posting from the start. Equally, Gough and Warner made no secret of the fact that they were delighted to be leaving the ship they hated so much (and had been in for over a year), said goodbye to Burney, and were sent to Halifax to await passage back to

121

Britain.

Stannard found the crew were very pro-Vichy and openly hostile towards them. They actually spat at them and physically stopped them from moving about the ship thus confining them to the radio room. *Surcouf* made a few short trips out into the Atlantic while the political cauldron at St Pierre bubbled away and during one of these Stannard remembers *Surcouf* getting out of control and diving far beyond its design limits.

Eventually *Surcouf* left St Pierre on January 11 for Halifax and during this voyage encountered very stormy weather which damaged part of her bridge superstructure, jamming the gun turret. By the time she reached harbour on January 14 she presented the dockyard with yet another long list of defects despite having only just completed an $800,000 overhaul.

At this point Stannard told Burney that:

We were so choked off [upset] by conditions on board
and our treatment by the French who hated us that
unless he got us off the ship we'd do something silly.
Burney said he understood how we felt and as an excuse
would tell the Admiralty we were too inexperienced and
find replacements for us.

On January 10 Burney sent a signal to the Admiralty asking for Gough and Warner to remain in Halifax, if they had not left there already, because he had found Stannard and Green too inexperienced and wanted them back. Burney amplified this in his report of January 16, saying Green was only twenty-one years old (in fact he was twenty-eight) and Stannard nineteen (he was twenty), adding that the:

Position of the two liaison ratings is fraught with
difficulties which demand not only years and character,
but also great patience, experience and independence.

As a result, when *Surcouf* got back to Halifax Gough and Warner were ordered to rejoin her and Stannard and Green left.

Stannard recalls that there was such bad feeling over this that Gough and Warner would not speak to them when they came back on board. It is ironic – and very poignant – that had transport become available earlier both Gough and Warner would have been safely on their way back to Britain and Stannard and Green would have had to remain on board irrespective of their feelings.

Burney's claim that Stannard and Green were too inexperienced to serve with him in *Surcouf* is remarkably unconvincing because both had served in submarines previously (which is more than Burney had) and Green had served in a French submarine earlier. A more logical, and charitable, explanation for Burney's irresponsible behaviour is that it was because of *his* inexperience that he felt he must have Gough and Warner back with him. But it was a terrible admission of his own failings and since he knew the pair were desperate to leave *Surcouf* the relationship between them must have become extremely awkward thereafter.

Burney had also made his views about *Surcouf* plain in meetings with De Wolff (Director of Operations with the RCN at Halifax) who was also very concerned about the efficiency of the submarine and the loyalties of her crew.[36] But as *Surcouf* was under the control of the Royal Navy it was not matter over which De Wolff could exercise any direct authority. However, De Wolff did pass on his views to Admiral George C Jones RN, at HMS *Forth*, which must have eventually got back to Horton in London.

The entry of Japan into the war gave Horton the opportunity to be rid of *Surcouf* by sending her out to Tahiti in the Pacific. Exactly who first suggested this idea is unclear from the records but on December 10 1941, before the St Pierre and Miquelon affair, a lot of rather pompous messages began passing between Free French naval headquarters in London and the French High Commissioner in Nouméa describing how valuable *Surcouf* with its 8-inch guns would be in defending them against the Japanese. Horton did nothing to discourage this enthusiasm his only concern being whether the dockyard at Halifax could get *Surcouf* into any sort of condition to make the journey, otherwise he would be stuck with the submarine on his hands.

On December 25 Horton cabled *Malabar*.

> Request you will sail *Surcouf* as soon as she is released from her present employment to Tahiti via Bermuda and Panama Canal.[37]

In his report to Horton of January 16 Burney reported that:

> Secret orders from the Admiralty arrived for *Surcouf* at St Pierre . . . sailing her for Halifax, Bermuda, Panama, Tahiti, and New Caledonia. On the following day an American newspaper reporter told me had heard *Surcouf* was sailing immediately for Panama, Tahiti, and New Caledonia and asked me if there was any truth in it. The time of our sailing from St Pierre [for Halifax] was generally known by the people of St Pierre . . . the captain has now put a notice up in the control room . . . that our movements are not to be disclosed ashore.

Surcouf remained in Halifax for the rest of January 1942 while the dockyard struggled to get her seaworthy again. Meanwhile *Malabar* was not anxious to have this vessel back in Bermuda and cabled the Admiralty on January 29:

> Present *U-boat* situation makes it undesirable for *Surcouf* to call at Bermuda. As there is no apparent reason for such a visit propose she proceed from Halifax direct to Panama Canal.[38]

On February 3 Halifax dockyard optimistically reported 'Defects *Surcouf* completed'[39] and the ship sailed straight for Bermuda where she arrived on February 7. During the voyage a major fault was discovered in one of the main electric motor armatures putting it out of action so that she could only dive on

one electric motor. Considering the number of times she had
gone out of control when submerging with both working, this
left her in an extremely hazardous situation since she could only
travel on the surface in an area where *Malabar* had already
warned German *U-boats* were active. The Bermuda dockyard
estimated that to dismantle the motor, remove the armature,
and repair it would take at least three months and bearing in
mind their lack of experience with submarines this was certainly
an optimistic calculation.

Even before *Surcouf* reached Bermuda the C-in-C, Admiral
Kennedy-Purvis, had started to take an interest in her future
because Burney had sent copies of all his earlier reports to *Malabar* which eventually ended up on Kennedy-Purvis's desk. At
first Kennedy-Purvis thought this young inexperienced officer
was being far too intemperate with his criticisms and sent for
Burney with a view to reprimanding him. However, despite
what must have been a daunting experience for a young sub-
lieutenant, Burney acquitted himself well and evidently impressed Kennedy-Purvis sufficiently for him to turn to Commander Guy Ridgeway RN, the senior naval intelligence officer
at *Malabar*, for advice.

After talking with Burney, Ridgeway decided to interrogate
Surcouf's crew and came to the conclusion that over half were
pro-Vichy and could not be fully trusted to serve the allied
cause.[40] Ridgeway gave his findings to Kennedy-Purvis who, on
February 5 1942, sent a 'Most Secret' signal to Horton:

After discussion with BNLO and from my experience of
Surcouf I am convinced that this most unsatisfactory
state of affairs is not in the least exaggerated.

The two main troubles are lack of interest and
incompetency . . . discipline is bad and the officers have
little control. I have no suggestions to make which are
likely to assist in eliminating these defects which I am
afraid are inherent.[41]

Surcouf is a large, complicated and indifferently
designed submarine [which] could only be of operational

value if manned by an exceptionally well-trained crew.
At present she is of no operational value and is little
short of a menace. For political reasons it may be
desirable to keep her in commission, but my view is that
she should proceed to UK and pay off.

Others shared the admiral's opinion. William King, who worked
in the cipher office at *Malabar*, remembers that the opinion was
that *Surcouf* was 'incredibly badly run and a useless ship' and
that Burney was very depressed about his job.[42]

Burney was now writing what was to be his last report, dated
February 10 1942, and as usual did not mince his words.

In the course of a conversation on submarine warfare
with the captain [Blaison] who claims a considerable
submarine experience, he made the following remark to
me: 'I often wonder how it is possible to identify a
friendly ship from a hostile ship simply by seeing her
through a periscope lens'. Since *Surcouf* came out of dry
dock she has carried out one crash dive only and that for
the benefit of her refit supervisors. Throughout the latest
voyage to Bermuda she did not even so much as make a
trim dive although the captain had told me that in the
event of meeting a *U-boat* . . . he would dive
immediately. Just before leaving Halifax I discovered . . .
that of our sixteen underwater listening microphones
[hydrophones] only seven were showing any signs of life
and even these could not be relied upon.[43]

The significance of this last comment is, of course, that without
hydrophones a submarine cannot detect the presence of other
vessels when submerged except by visual contact through the
periscope.

Burney then told how *Surcouf*'s navigator, who had attended
the French naval academy, had asked him for a new set of charts
because the ones he was using were four months out of date and
he did not know how to correct them. Burney got him a new set

and showed him how to do this from the *Notice to Mariners* regularly issued by the Admiralty.

Burney's final remarks were reserved for Gough and Warner who he said: 'are treated at times in a way that can only be described as gratuitously unpleasant'[44] and in view of their excellent service asked that they be considered for promotion to petty officer.

Burney's reports were in marked contrast to those regularly submitted by Ortoli, and now Blaison, to the Free French naval headquarters in London. These tended to deal with peripheral matters such as who had visited the submarine or who the captain had dinner with and there were only fleeting references to problems of morale. Nothing was said about the endless mishaps so it is perhaps not surprising that Muselier had a rather different impression of *Surcouf*'s capabilities than Horton.

The 'Most Secret' message from Kennedy-Purvis was an unwelcome arrival on Horton's desk but could not be ignored because of his position and seniority, and also because he had sent copies to virtually everyone of any importance in the Admiralty from the First Lord downwards although – not surprisingly – no copy went to the Free French. The very last thing Horton wanted was for *Surcouf* to return to Britain with the idea of paying off which would immediately involve endless arguments with Muselier, de Gaulle, and probably Churchill. Horton wanted *Surcouf* as far away as possible: Tahiti was an ideal choice since it was controlled by the French and when *Surcouf* inevitably broke down, they could have the problem of repairing her.

The day after receiving the signal from Bermuda, February 6, Horton sent a message to the Admiralty and Bermuda:

> The CO [commanding officer] of *Surcouf* is a seaman
> who knows his job and his ship well. The First
> Lieutenant is a good officer and experienced in
> submarines. The engineer and key ratings are well
> experienced. The crew have suffered [from] inaction and
> anti-British propaganda in Canada. To get any results

from these Free French they must be kept in the front
line and kept there. I am sure Commander Cabanier at
Tahiti can make use of *Surcouf* and in an active war area
and . . . I consider *Surcouf* may be of considerable use.
Surcouf occupies a peculiar position in French naval
mentality and the Free French would hate to pay her off.
In any case a large crew would be required for care and
maintenance and she would be a nuisance in this
country. I strongly recommend *Surcouf* proceeding as
already ordered.[45]

By any standards this was an amazing message, especially coming from someone so experienced as Horton, and must have
been written with his tongue firmly in his cheek. With the ex-
ception of the penultimate sentence it was untrue and Horton
knew it.

While Blaison was indeed a competent sailor in a conventional submarine he could not get *Surcouf* to work properly
because of its inherent design defects and his acute shortage of
trained personnel. Since joining the Free French navy in July
1940 *Surcouf* had made just four operational voyages plus the
unauthorized mission to St Pierre. On each occasion there had
been a series of major disasters caused by a combination of poor
command and technical problems. All the BNLOs had complained of the lack of discipline, poor watchkeeping, failure to
use recognition signals when challenged, and drunkenness.

Surcouf had not fired its guns or torpedoes since the war
began and every BNLO had doubted whether it possessed the
ability to do so. Horton knew that because of *Surcouf*'s slow
diving time she was useless in a war situation where the enemy
had air patrols and, since the Japanese had demonstrated their
ability to use carrier-borne aircraft to disastrous effect, *Surcouf*
would have been at risk from the moment any attack on Tahiti
took place.

While Horton's message was on its way to Bermuda,
Kennedy-Purvis, sent another message to him and the
Admiralty:

Satisfactory repairs can only be effected by removal of
main armature, estimated time if undertaken at Bermuda
three months, not, repetition not, desirable to undertake
work at Bermuda owing to other commitments.
Commanding officer . . . is anxious about effect on
morale of crew if further prolonged time spent in
dockyard . . . I do not consider temporary repairs a
satisfactory solution. Under circumstances I propose ship
proceed UK and pay off.[46]

Horton replied to this on February 7:

I consider that even if temporary repairs at Bermuda
prove unsatisfactory on passage to Tahiti *Surcouf* can still
dive using one shaft. At Tahiti her 8-inch guns would
provide a valuable addition to defence of this or other
islands. If it was found necessary to pay her off this
should be done at Tahiti where her crew could add to
strength of local defence force, a few of the better
officers and key ratings being sent back to UK to act as
spares for Free French submarines. Propose therefore
that temporary repairs be made at Bermuda.

Again this was an extraordinary message. The idea that the
Bermuda dockyard could effect temporary repairs was nonsense. The *Surcouf* had two electric motors, made by CGE at
Nancy, each of 1700 hp and were massive affairs. The armature
of an electric motor is the central revolving core and the insulation on one of these had broken down rendering the motor
inoperable. It was the same fault that had plagued *Surcouf* since
she was launched, as Ortoli explained after the war:

Our principal motor armatures gave us a lot of trouble
and the fragile state of the armatures' insulation had its
inevitable effect on *Surcouf*'s efficiency.[47]

The only way to repair the faulty armature was to remove the

129

top half of the stator casing and lift out the complete armature, which also meant removing the deck above the engine room, and then sending it to a workshop capable of rewinding the faulty section. It was a large and complex task that could only be undertaken at a dockyard equipped to handle submarines but, until it was done, *Surcouf* could only use one of its propellers. Horton knew this better than anyone and Bermuda's lack of repair facilities was borne out by the number of British submarines now in the Portsmouth navy yard undergoing repair. Horton also knew that *Surcouf*'s 8-inch guns would be of little value in defending Tahiti from the Japanese – even assuming they could fire – and in any case she only had 150 rounds per gun after which there were no further supplies.

But it is when Horton talks about paying off *Surcouf* in Tahiti that his thinking becomes clearer. Effectively he was saying that having got this useless vessel out in the middle of the Pacific, where it would arrive with its usual long list of defects (including the defective motor), because there were even less dockyard facilities than Bermuda the submarine would automatically become an immovable hulk that the French themselves would be forced to pay off, thus relieving him of the responsibility and Churchill the embarrassment.

Although this was a very astute move it overlooked two things. First, Horton was proposing that this very large submarine with its defective motor would travel the 1700 miles from Bermuda to the Panama Canal entirely on the surface, both during the day and night, through an area in which Bermuda had already warned German *U-boats* were active. Horton knew from Burney's report that nearly all *Surcouf*'s hydrophones were out of order, watchkeeping was virtually non-existent, and, of course, she had no radar. Because of *Surcouf*'s condition the very least Horton could have arranged was for her to be escorted by another surface vessel as far as Panama. This he did not do, and perhaps *Malabar* had no corvettes to spare, although the French corvette *Mimosa* was still at Halifax. Later it was to be argued that submarines are not normally escorted over such long distances but the circumstances in this instance were so peculiar that an escort would have been quite proper. It certainly seemed that Horton was determined to be rid of *Surcouf* whatever the risks involved.

Second, the ramifications of all this were not lost on the crew. After a long time wandering vaguely around the Atlantic encountering a series of disasters and spending three months in an American dockyard, they were now to sail on a long voyage to Panama on the surface across seas where *U-boats* had sunk many ships recently. From there they were to go to Tahiti across the Pacific (also on the surface) to repulse attacks from the Japanese who had apparently just wiped out the US Pacific Fleet with amazing ease. It was hardly a mission likely to inspire confidence or raise morale.

With the die now cast Kennedy-Purvis raised with Horton the vexed question of whose command *Surcouf* would come under when it reached Tahiti. Originally it had been planned she would be under the control of C-in-C Eastern Fleet but it was subsequently decided to place her under the direct orders of the Free French naval Pacific division in Tahiti on board the destroyer *Triomphant*. On February 12 Kennedy-Purvis then dealt with the future of the liaison staff:

The question of the BNLO and ratings also causes me concern . . . if *Surcouf* is to be employed on local defence of Free French territory [in the Pacific] consider liaison personnel should be withdrawn without [a] relief. Liaison personnel have carried out a very difficult and most disheartening task in a most praiseworthy manner and are deserving of consideration.[48]

Horton immediately replied on February 13:

Entirely agree with proposal that British liaison personnel be withdrawn and suggest this being done at Bermuda or Panama.[49]

It does not appear that anyone at *Malabar* discussed this with

131

Burney, because in Warner's last letter to his wife, written late in the evening of February 11, he obliquely explains they are on the move:

> I'll send a cable to let you know where to write. . . it's no use having letters chasing all round the place for I suppose those of the last five months are being waffled by kangaroos, ostriches, and snakes.[50]

His wife and family assumed the last sentence was meant to indicate *Surcouf* was off to Australia since their previous letters had reached him, and they knew from a short item in the London *Evening Standard* for January 8 1942 that he had been involved in the St Pierre affair.

However, Warner's letter two days earlier on February 9 did contain one rather puzzling paragraph when he referred to having visited Boston since Christmas (which would be when *Surcouf* returned to Halifax from St Pierre). Evidently some friends there had told him that his sketches were so good that there could be a future for him as an artist after the war. Warner then wrote:

> It's an astounding fact that being so fundamentally and essentially British, I realize my best friends on whom I could count in *any* [original emphasis] situation are American which rather shakes me but it's true.[51]

The tenor of this comment is so totally different to the rest of his letters that read in the light of some of the unpleasant rumours concerning Warner and Gough that subsequently circulated (see Chapter 9) his family wondered if this remark was an intimation that he wanted to stay in America. However, a more likely explanation is that, while in Portsmouth, Warner had been well looked after by the Americans with their typical generosity and had been much impressed by their lack of concern for either social class or military rank.

Nevertheless when Warner and Gough left the comfort of

'Benker' on the morning of February 12 to board *Surcouf* they can hardly have been looking forward to the voyage. Even Rose Baker noticed something was wrong and, some months later after the loss of *Surcouf* had been announced, wrote to Mrs Warner: 'I knew something was wrong the day they left. This was the first time they left without a smile.'[52]

Burney was also very worried about what might happen to *Surcouf* once they left Bermuda. Burney had twice dated twenty-two-year-old Mary Ridgeway (now Mrs Henry Smythe), the eldest daughter of Guy Ridgeway, and he took her on board *Surcouf* to show her around. Even now after fifty years, Mrs Smythe recalls with enormous sorrow how unhappy Burney was:

> He was the saddest man I've ever met and longed to get off *Surcouf*. I have never felt so sorry for anyone in my life. He told me the crew were absolute stinkers and he was scared stiff. As we said our last goodbye he said: 'When we sail I will never come back – they [the French crew] will throw me overboard'. It was like shaking hands with a dead man already standing on the edge of his grave.[53]

When Mary got back home and told her father she had met Burney, much to her surprise he:

> Fairly blew up and for the first time in my life became really angry. He said I should not have gone on board [*Surcouf*] and should not meet Burney again. I was amazed at his attitude.[54]

Fifty years later, when told for the first time of the claim that her father might have been involved in a plan to destroy *Surcouf* (see Chapter 9) Mrs Smythe wondered if her father's sudden anger may have been a guilty conscience.

Mary's younger sister, June (now Mrs June Stanton), worked at the airbase at Darrels Island and vividly recalls how worried her father was about *Surcouf* and, although he never discussed the details of his work with them, it became plain enough from their conversations in the evening that the problem of what to do with *Surcouf* was his main preoccupation.[55]

Miss René Brass (now Mrs Northover) lived with her parents at *Malabar*, and taught French at the Bermuda High School for girls:

> I remember seeing little groups of French sailors with their flat white caps, red pom-poms on top, and the Free French cross pinned to their uniforms, wandering about Ireland Island. My mother had about a dozen of them to tea at our house and, to my utter dismay, I found the French I so proudly spoke was quite unlike their *patois* which was all they spoke. It was like another language. I think most of them were from Brittany. After tea we took them walking around the prettier parts of Ireland Island. I remember when I realized they were trying to tell me all was not well on board the *Surcouf*. It seemed they did not like or trust their officers and they did not want to go back to sea, and were very afraid of something. When I later went on board *Surcouf* the men took me down to the galley, away from the officers, to talk to me. It was hard for me to follow all they said, but it seemed they believed once they sailed they would never return. But I was too young and inexperienced to understand such things and so she did sail with all her men.[56]

Malabar gave *Surcouf* a route to Panama requiring the vessel to pass through the Caicos Passage (between the islands of Grand Caicos and Great Inagua, north-east of Cuba), then through the Windward Passage (between Cuba and Haiti),[57] maintaining a speed, which would not be more than 10 knots bearing in mind that she only had one shaft operating, enabling her to arrive off Colon at 8 am on the morning of February 19. No details of any other ships in the area were given to *Surcouf*, but a copy of her

134

sailing orders was passed to the US Navy.

Surcouf had been due to sail from Bermuda on February 9 but last-minute defects postponed the departure, and it was not until 3 pm on February 12 1942 that Burney, Warner and Gough watched Ireland Island disappear into the distance. Shortly after *Surcouf* had sailed, a signal arrived from London agreeing that the British naval liaison team could either leave the submarine in Bermuda, or when it arrived in Colon.[58]

But Burney and his team never got the message and, after *Surcouf* disappeared over the horizon south of Bermuda no sight or trace of her, not a scrap of wreckage, or a member of her crew was ever seen again. In her wake she left behind a tangled web of intrigue and rumour that was to create one of the most controversial maritime disasters of World War II.

NOTES

1. Interview with Roger Burney's sister, Mrs Joan Adams, Hereford, June 1990, who very kindly made available her brother's photographs.

2. Christopher Burney joined Special Operations Executive (SOE) and was parachuted into France on May 31 1942 to join the *Autogiro* network. Captured by the Germans, Christopher was tortured and sent to Buchenwald but happily survived the war, was awarded the MBE, and later became a successful merchant banker. *The Dungeon Democracy*, Christopher Burney (Heinemann, 1945), *Solitary Confinement*, Christopher Burney (Macmillan, 1952), and *SOE in France*, MRD Foot (HMSO, 1966), 194–5.

3. Fortunately, Dorothy Burney had a private income of £200 a year enabling her to rent a large farmhouse in Worcestershire for £50 a year, although the gardener's wages were £80 a year.

4. Annual fees at Wellington College were then £140 a year reduced to £125 for officers' sons. An exhibition was worth only £10 a year, but a foundation was worth £115 a year leaving Mrs Burney only £10 to pay. The author is most grateful to Robert Sopwith, the Wellington College archivist, for his valuable help.

5. The author is most grateful for the help received from the Master of Peterhouse, The Revd Professor Henry Chadwick DD FBA.

6. The letters from Roger Burney to Peter Pears were kindly made available to the author by the Trustees of the Pears–Britten Archives.

7. In 1962 Britten dedicated his *War Requiem* to Roger Burney, Captain Piers Dunkerley RM, David Gill RN, and Lieutenant Michael Halliday RNZNVR.

8. The *Athenia* was sunk by the *U-30* with the loss of 128 lives on September 4 1939 the day after the outbreak of war. The attack was in contravention not only of the London Naval Agreement but also Hitler's orders that passenger ships were not to be attacked so the Germans put out a crude story that the Royal Navy had sunk the liner to provide an excuse to arm merchant ships.

9. Record Group 181, Box 43, File EF13/L9-3(161) (National Archives, Waltham, Mass, USA).

10. As late as February 1942 the Portsmouth navy yard's workshops were still working on specially made spares for *Surcouf*.

11. 'This will acknowledge for and on behalf of the United Kingdom completion to my entire satisfaction of work requisitioned on Repair Request No. 161.' (National Archives, Waltham, Mass, USA).

12. It is noteworthy that the *Time* magazine reporter was evidently told the aircraft was still on board *Surcouf* although it had been destroyed in 1940 in Plymouth.

13. Message No. 1076, FO 371/28453 (PRO, Kew).

14. *Ibid.*

15. *Ibid.*

16. From the log of the *Atlantic* sent to Lieutenant Commander Michael Wilson RN (Ret'd), Naval Historical Branch, London, letter to author March 5 1986, ref: D/NHB/3/3/552.

17. ADM 199/829 (PRO, Kew).

18. *Sundry Times*, Frank Giles (John Murray, 1986), 31.

19. Pears–Britten Archives.

20. *Newfoundland in the North Atlantic World*, Peter Neary (McGill Queen's University Press, Canada, 1989,) 134–5, and FO 371/31873 (PRO, Kew).

21. *The Call to Honour*, Charles de Gaulle (Collins, 1955), 217.

22. In theory the Free French authorities in London had their own communications system and codes but in practice as their messages went over Admiralty lines, their security was inevitably compromised.

23. Morton had first met Churchill on the western front in World War I and from 1929 to 1939 had been head of the Industrial Intelligence Centre, the cover name of a government agency responsible for discovering the true nature of Germany's war plans. Morton had covertly, and illegally, fed Churchill throughout the 1930s secret information about the Nazis so that Churchill could harass the government about their lack of defence spending. Unlike Roosevelt, Churchill insisted that he see the raw decrypts of all important intercepted material rather than summaries. As a result Churchill knew more about the enemy's intentions than his own military leaders.

24. FO 371/31873 (PRO, Kew).

25. *Ibid.*

26. Interview with Vice Admiral HG De Wolff CBE DSO DSC CD RCN

(Ret'd), Ottawa, November 1990.

27. Burney's report January 16 1942, ADM 199/829 (PRO).
28. *Submarine Warfare: Monsters and Midgets*, Richard Compton-Hall(Blandford Press, 1985), 54.
29. FO 371/31873 (PRO, Kew).
30. PSF File, Boxes 4, 41, 42, and 90 (St Pierre & Miquelon) (Franklin D Roosevelt Library, New York).
31. ADM 199/829 (PRO, Kew).
32. Boyer interview, 1990.
33. Originally one of the US destroyers supplied in 1940.
34. After Boyer took command of *L-27* the previous captain was appointed commander of HMS *P-511* and ordered to sail for Halifax escorted by a Canadian corvette. On the way the corvette lost contact with *P-511* which ran into a southbound convoy and was attacked and sunk with all her crew. Disasters of this nature were, sadly, not uncommon even with the most efficient submarines.
35. Interview with Lawrence Stannard, Kent, June 1990.
36. De Wolff interview.
37. Message No. 3755 (Vincennes Archives, Paris).
38. Message No. 4181 (Vincennes Archives, Paris).
39. Message No. 4277 (Vincennes Archives, Paris).
40. Interview with Mrs Henry Smythe (formerly Miss Mary Ridgeway), Charleston, South Carolina, November 1990.
41. Message No. 898, Folio 22, ADM 199/829 (PRO, Kew).
42. Interview with Mr William King, Bermuda, November 1990.
43. ADM 199/829 (PRO, Kew).
44. *Ibid.*
45. Message No. 926, Folio 23, ADM 199/829 (PRO, Kew).
46. Message No. 911, Folio 35, ADM 199/829 (PRO, Kew).
47. Ortoli letter, 1960 (Vincennes Archives, Paris).
48. Message No. 977, Folio 32, ADM 199/829 (PRO, Kew).
49. Message No. 987, Folio 34, *ibid.*
59. Warner private papers.
51. *Ibid.*
52. *Ibid.*
53. Mrs Henry Smythe interview.
54. *Ibid.*
55. Interview with Mrs June Stanton (formerly Miss June Ridgeway), Bermuda, November 1990.
56. Interview with Mrs Guy Northover (formerly Miss René Brass), Bermuda, November 1990.
57. Message No. 4820 (Vincennes Archives, Paris).
58. ADM 199/829 (PRO, Kew).

CHAPTER 7

COLLISION COURSE

At 4.40 pm in the late afternoon of February 18 1942, local time, Captain Henry Johnson stood on the port wing of the bridge of the 6762-ton American freighter *Thompson Lykes*. He watched the pilot slowly make his way down the ladder to the cutter lazily rolling in the swell off the Cristobal breakwater at the Atlantic entrance to the Panama Canal and, as it pulled away, the pilot gave a friendly wave to Johnson who waved back.

Johnson lived in Kentucky Street, New Orleans, and had forty years of seagoing experience, holding a Master's licence since 1921. The *Thompson Lykes* was a new vessel and Johnson had been her captain since the ship was first commissioned on April 25 1941. She was now part of the Lykes Brothers Steamship Company's fleet with its headquarters in New Orleans. Following the outbreak of war in December 1941 the ship had been time-chartered by the US Army although it was the US Navy authorities in Panama who issued the necessary sailing instructions.

For Johnson this was a perfectly straightforward voyage being the return half of a round trip from New Orleans to Cristobal that had begun on February 6. In the morning he had called in at the US Army's transport service offices at Cristobal and Lieutenant Lamphier had given him his written orders requiring him to proceed to Guantanamo Bay in Cuba. There he was to report to the US naval commandant and load a cargo of sugar and then continue on to New Orleans to discharge at the US Army base. Shortly after lunch Johnson met with Lieutenant Commander Tawes USN, the naval port director, who typed up in his presence written sailing orders instructing Johnson to take the normal trade route that would pass between Jamaica and Navassa Island, leaving him to decide his speed according to sea conditions. There was no mention of any other vessels being in the area of his route.

The *Thompson Lykes* was 418 foot long with a beam of 60 feet and a fully loaded draft of 28 feet. Its gross tonnage was 6763 and maximum speed through calm water was 15 knots. On this leg of the trip the ship was only lightly loaded with army cargo drawing 11 feet forward and 27 feet aft, giving a mean draft of only 14 feet and also making the bow rather higher in the water than normal. On board was a crew of forty-five with twenty-three members of the US Army manning the guns.

As the pilot cutter disappeared Johnson walked back into the bridge house where Andrew Thompson, the mate, and George Atwell, the helmsman, waited. Johnson told Thompson to set course 028° with their maximum speed of 15 knots since the weather was good with a gentle northerly breeze and a moderate north-easterly swell. Thompson pushed the engine telegraph to 'Full'; there was an answering jangle from the engine room followed by a faint shudder as the single-screw propeller started to turn and the ship began to plough through the leaden seas out into the tropical evening.

The bridge instruments and equipment gleamed as befitted a ship so new but already the war – only ten weeks old – had taken its toll and some of the best seamen had been drafted to serve with the US Navy. Their places had been taken by untrained conscripts from the US Army's 58th Coast Artillery Transport Detachment most of whom had never been to sea before. Officially they were supposed to man the anti-aircraft guns and keep lookout but Johnson had little faith in their abilities.

Johnson checked that John Fitzpatrick, an experienced seaman, was stationed in the crow's-nest. It was the highest lookout

139

point in the ship and was also protected against the weather and with a telephone to the bridge. Ideally he would have liked to place another seaman right up in the bow but, as there was no telephone there, the lookout would have no way of telling the bridge if he saw anything.

Silence descended on the bridge with each man wrapped in his own thoughts. War had suddenly made what had previously been a relatively simple and safe job extremely hazardous. Already German *U-boats* were operating in the Caribbean and several American merchant ships had been sunk. Yet so far the US Navy had not introduced any convoy system and unescorted freighters were still sailing to peacetime schedules. As the mate peered ahead into the dusk only the ticking of the automatic log and the gentle creaking of the superstructure broke the silence.

The mate, Thompson, had been at sea for thirty years. He came from a Danish seafaring family and two years earlier had obtained his master's certificate. Between Johnson and Thompson they represented seventy years of seagoing experience. A few miles out a swell started and the first wave broke over the bow; another reason you could not put a lookout there. Johnson peered over Atwell's shoulder at the gyro repeater which showed 027°, making a true course of 028°, and then went into his office which was just behind the bridge.

For the next hour and a half the *Thompson Lykes* ploughed on steadily through the now heavy swell until at 6.30 pm Thompson ordered all lights – including the navigation lights – to be extinguished. Leaving the captain on the bridge Thompson made a careful inspection of the ship to ensure no portholes had been left uncovered. Now the vessel merged with the sea into a grey unidentifiable mass. Darkness in the Caribbean comes quickly with only a brief moment of twilight. By 7 pm total blackness enveloped the sky, sea, and ship.

By now the swell was getting heavier and Johnson decided to reduce speed to 13 knots. Time passed slowly but there was little small talk. Everyone knew that out there in the Stygian darkness lay unexpected danger. At 8 pm watches were changed and Johnson called the mate over to examine the chart. They decided in view of the deteriorating weather to change course and instead of passing Navassa Island make for Guantanamo direct. As they were under strict radio silence there was no way in which Johnson could advise the US Navy at Cristobal, but in any case the course was for him alone to decide. Johnson and Thompson returned to the bridge and gave Atwell at the helm orders to change course to 022°.

The vigil was interrupted at 9 pm when the bridge telephone buzzed with a message from the radio operator. Johnson made his way to the radio room and was handed a coded signal from the Canal Zone. He went back to his office, twirled the dial of his safe, and took out his copy of the US Merchant Shipping code. Adjusting the desk lamp he began decoding the cipher groups. It turned out to be a simple message from the US Army in Cristobal ordering him to go to Cienfuegos instead of Guantanamo. Johnson checked the chart and returned to the bridge where he told Thompson the news and then gave a course correction to 355° on the gyro. Ponderously the ship swung round to its new destination.

Johnson returned to his office and began working his way through the mass of paperwork war had generated. Army forms, navy forms, Lykes Steamship forms. There seemed more paper than he had cargo. A little later the steward arrived with Johnson's supper. As he began to eat, the bulkhead clock showed 10.25 pm.

On the bridge all was quiet. The bridge clock swept silently to 10.28 pm. Only the faint glow from the compass broke the darkness. The night was so dark the ship seemed afloat in a world of its own.

Suddenly Atwell saw a bright white light moving up and down out to the right. 'Light on the starboard bow,' he yelled. Thompson rushed over to the bridge windows on that side and the same moment the crow's-nest telephone rang and Fitzpatrick squawked: 'White light, one point to starboard'. 'I see it, I see it,' shouted Thompson, 'full rudder port, emergency.'

'Wheel is full left,' responded Atwell as the spokes flew round in his hands.

An age passed. The crow's-nest telephone rang again. 'Light dead ahead,' came the message.

'Christ – it's going across the bows,' yelled Thompson, 'full rudder starboard – now.'

Atwell deftly spun the wheel round the opposite way: 'Right full rudder,' he called. Inexorably the *Thompson Lykes* ploughed on. The bridge clock showed 10.29 pm.

Seconds later the whole vessel shuddered. To some it was as if a giant hand had reached out of the darkness and for a brief moment stopped the *Thompson Lykes* in her tracks before letting her go on her way. Others thought the ship had ridden up over something. Another said it was as if the ship was running up on to a beach.

Johnson burst out of his office. 'What the hell was that?'

'I dunno – a light – there was this white light', began Thompson, 'out to starboard. I went hard port but then . . . '

Suddenly there was a loud explosion and a brilliant sheet of flame shot up from the water on both sides of the bow like a huge flash bulb starkly illuminating the ship. It was so dazzling that those on the bridge long accustomed to the darkness were blinded.

'The engines. Have you stopped?' shouted Johnson. 'No sir, there wasn't . . .' began Thompson. 'Stop engines,' yelled Johnson and Thompson yanked back the telegraph. The reply clanged back from the engine room.

Outside the flames had gone leaving the scene once again in total darkness. 'Someone in the water,' called Private Dohrman Henke from his lookout position. Thompson and Johnson pushed through the portside door out on to the wing bridge. The air was full of a strong smell of oil.

'Down there . . . there,' yelled Henke from his position above them on the hurricane deck. But in the swirling waters rushing past the ship only a brief glimpse of something white could be seen. Some faint voices shouting 'help'. Then nothing more.

Thompson and the master stared into the darkness. 'Did you see anything?' they asked each other simultaneously. Neither replied. There was nothing to say. There was nothing to see.

142

'What did you see?' yelled Johnson to Henke. It was Henke's first trip at sea and he was scared and seasick. 'Dunno sir. Saw a light . . a white light . . . then . . . I think we scraped a sub . . . it went past us on this side.'

Johnson's long experience took control. He went back into the bridge house. 'Mr Mate have the forepeak sounded for water. Check the bottom tanks. And send a man up to turn on the searchlight. Helm, come left and slow speed ahead.' The silver finger of light probed the darkness over the heavy swell highlighting the flecked waves as the ship slowly began to retrace its steps.

The crew of the *Thompson Lykes* lined the rails and peered down into the darkness. But there was nothing. No wreckage. No bodies. No survivors. Just some heavy thick fuel oil that a tanker might carry.

After a while Thompson reported back to the ship's carpenter that the forepeak was sound. Johnson nodded: 'It's weird. We hit a ship yet there's no wreckage. Not a scrap of timber, piece of liferaft. Nothing. What sort of ship could it have been?'

Atwell still at the helm said it was no ordinary ship because otherwise he would have seen something against the horizon. Therefore it must have been very low in the water, much lower than the bow of the *Thompson Lykes*. With the searchlight playing over the water the ship continued to slowly circle the area. All the navigation lights were turned on to make it easier for any survivor to see them.

Lieutenant Kuns who was in charge of the army gun crews arrived on the bridge and reported that all he could get from his men was that they had seen something long and round – one said like a cigar – sliding past the ship and disappearing into the darkness astern. Plainly the only vessel that matched that description was a submarine on the surface. But whose? Johnson had been told nothing about any American submarines in the area so could it have been a German *U-boat* recharging its batteries on the surface?

Johnson decided to break radio silence and sent a short message to the naval authorities at Cristobal saying he had accidentally struck an unidentified vessel which he believed was a submarine. After a while there was a reply ordering him to remain in the area until daylight and continue the search for survivors. When dawn came Johnson checked his position and estimated the collision had occurred at 10°40'N 79°31'W, or about seventy-five miles north-east of Cristobal.

At around 10.45 am that morning the destroyer USS *Tattnall*, which was patrolling the area, appeared and Johnson signalled what had happened. Later they were joined by the destroyer USS *Barry* and while the two warships continued to search the area the *Thompson Lykes* left to return to Cristobal. Tired and weary Johnson ordered the helmsman to turn the ship to the south-west and retrace their course back to the Panama Canal. Johnson walked out on to the wing of the bridge and looked back at their tumbling wake. Apart from the slight oil slick there was nothing to show that anything had ever happened. It was as if a ghost had walked past them in the night.

NOTES

The conversations in this chapter have been reconstructed from the transcript of the official inquiry (Record Group No. 041, Civil Reference Branch, National Archives, Washington, DC).

CHAPTER 8
THE INQUIRY

The *Thompson Lykes* arrived off the Cristobal breakwater at
2.31 pm on the afternoon of February 19 1942. A navy cutter
came out to take Johnson to headquarters leaving Thompson
and the pilot to finally dock the vessel at Pier 6 at 4.20 pm.

Johnson reached naval headquarters at around 3.15 pm and,
while he was explaining what had happened, news came in that
the French submarine *Surcouf* was overdue. *Surcouf* had been
told to wait off the entrance to the Canal until daylight and
arrive at 8 am but nothing had been seen of her nor had her captain broken radio silence to indicate they were in any sort of
trouble. The two reports sounded ominously connected so the
British Consular Shipping Adviser (CSA) in Colon was told
and, shortly afterwards, he sent a 'Most Secret' telegram to the
Admiralty in London:

> French cruiser-sub *Surcouf* not repetition not arrived.
> *Thompson Lykes* USA army transport northbound
> convoy yesterday returned after collision with
> unidentified vessel which apparently sank at once at
> 2230R 18th February in latitude 010 degs 40 North
> longitude 079 degs 30 West. She searched the vicinity
> until 0830 today 19th February but no survivors or
> wreckage. Only sign was oil. Considerable bow damage

made to *Thompson Lykes* at fore foot.[1]

Considering the haste with which this information had been col-
lated it was hardly surprising that there were some errors in his
report. The *Thompson Lykes* had not been part of a convoy but
was sailing alone nor had any member of the crew actually seen
the other vessel sink. But it was small discrepancies such as
these that were later to be magnified out of all proportion as
proof that something sinister had happened.

Shortly afterwards the *Thompson Lykes* was examined by surveyors from the American Bureau of Shipping as she lay afloat
alongside Pier 6.[2] To enable them to check the damage her ballast was shifted so as to raise her bow out of the water. They reported on February 25 that although some plating had been
damaged, a few of the frames badly distorted, and one double-
bottom fuel tank holed there was nothing substantially wrong
with the vessel.[3] The surveyors recommended that after some
temporary repairs – which involved pouring cement into the
damaged compartments – the *Thompson Lykes* be allowed to
continue its voyage back to its home port of New Orleans where
full repairs could be carried out in dry dock. The Bureau estimated the cost of the damage at $38,000.

Meanwhile on February 20 the CSA sent a further message:

USA authorities investigated Master's report and wide
air search carried out. Understand unofficially that
preliminary enquiries point to likelihood of sunken vessel
being an armed launch. 15th naval district apparently not
informed of route or speed of *Surcouf* from which to
estimate position.[4]

This brought a swift response from BAD in Washington who
stated that the *Surcouf*'s route and expected time of arrival off
Colon had indeed been passed to the Americans.[5]

On February 21 the CSA sent the Admiralty another message
outlining the circumstances of the collision and also gave some
details of the damage to the *Thompson Lykes*:

146

From personal observation 15-yard distance nature of
damage to US ship points to other not being surface craft
as upper two-third stem post and pole plate not
damaged.

US authorities now severely limit communication to
ships and preserve close secrecy. Nothing has been told
me officially but local [US] naval intelligence persuaded
by US Navy port captain allowed me unofficially to read
. . . statements [of collision]. They know I am reporting
facts and inference to you but have not informed their
superiors of my reading statements. Do not know if
Master [of *Thompson Lykes*] warned he might meet
French s/m *Surcouf*.[6]

The CSA added that apparently the *Thompson Lykes* was showing no lights at the time, whereas British and other allied merchant ships leaving the Canal area showed dim navigational light
while in the Caribbean.

By February 23 the CSA in Colon was reasonably certain that
the vessel sunk was *Surcouf* and asked if he should make a
formal application to the Americans for a board of inquiry that
he should attend. Back in London his message was digested by
John Higham of the Admiralty's Military Department who
minuted:

While there seems no obligation on the US to hold an
. . . inquiry, it is clearly desirable that the incident should
be thoroughly thrashed out and the . . . [Americans] . . .
are the right people to do it. As the board may well
make findings against the . . . master [of the *Thompson
Lykes*], there is a chance that the Free French may wish
to prefer a financial claim against the guilty party, we
shall have to tread carefully in suggesting that any British
authority be present.[7]

A handwritten footnote to this memorandum[8] suggested that instead of having a representative at the official inquiry he would

be called only an observer, presumably to downgrade any British involvement. Three days later the Admiralty sent Horton a short note asking for his views and pointing out that, as German submarines were active in the Caribbean, a merchant ship sighting one would automatically try and ram it, although on this occasion it was not clear if the ramming was accidental or deliberate. The Admiralty did not think an inquiry would achieve much, except to satisfy the feelings of the Free French, and the only important matter to determine was if *Malabar* had told the American Navy about *Surcouf*'s voyage.

During the next seven months a long, and sometimes bitter, wrangle ensued between the British, American, and Free French over the inquiry into the loss of *Surcouf*. Before examining this in detail it is important to set the affair in the context of early 1942 when the war had reached its peak of intensity around the world.

On the eastern front the Russians had suffered casualties of over 250,000 during a series of battles in the Ukraine; in the Far East 100,000 British and Commonwealth troops had been forced to surrender in humiliating circumstances following the fall of Singapore;[9] American forces were on the retreat throughout the Pacific, and naval losses had been very large; merchant seamen were being lost in their hundreds each week in convoys to Russia, across the Atlantic, and in the Mediterranean; the RAF might lose over 300 aircrew in a single night's raid on Germany; the same number were being killed in one air raid on Britain; and the Royal Navy often lost a submarine every week, usually by enemy action but sometimes by accident.

Set against this depressing backdrop the loss of *Surcouf*, irrespective of her size and the fact it was not by enemy action, was not specially significant to Horton or anyone else who had to deal with the realities of war on a daily basis, nor was there time to devote to a detailed investigation that might have been possible in peacetime. Nevertheless, for the Free French *Surcouf* always occupied a place in their thinking quite disproportionate to the vessel's real importance, and it was this inability to put *Surcouf*'s loss in its correct perspective that generated the belief that anything that could not be explained about her disappearance must be part of an evil conspiracy. Not surprisingly, as they persisted with this view, there was considerable exasperation on the part of the Admiralty and the US Navy.

On February 24, Captain Moret of the Free French navy wrote to John Higham at the Admiralty's Military Branch that:

> The accidental loss of *Surcouf* is an extremely serious blow for the Free French naval forces. For this reason I attach great importance to the fact that the maximum light should be shed on the circumstances of this accident . . . kindly take the necessary steps for the American authorities to be asked to convene a board of inquiry . . . and in particular that the deck log of the *Thompson Lykes* be communicated to us as soon as possible.[10]

Meanwhile the Navy Department in Washington had sent the secretary of state a short report about the loss of *Surcouf*:

> The enclosed data on the . . . *Surcouf* is forwarded with the suggestion that it be transmitted to the Free French authorities. Although the Commandant of the 15th naval district [Panama] apparently believes that the evidence shows that the *Surcouf* was sunk by collision with the *Thompson Lykes* it is desired to point out that the evidence is circumstantial and there is a possibility that *Surcouf* may have been sunk in some other way.[11]

Adolf Berle, assistant secretary at the State Department, sent the Navy's report to Adrien Tixier, head of the Free French delegation in Washington, on March 2 repeating the qualification about the manner of her sinking. That same day Captain GD Belben RN, at the British Embassy in Washington, asked Commander LR McDowell USN at the Navy Department to set up a formal inquiry. Two days later on March 4 Churchill wrote to Muselier:

> It is with profound regret that I have learnt of the loss of

the *Surcouf* and of her gallant crew under the command of Captain Blaison. You must share the sadness I feel in that *Surcouf* was not sunk in action but by an accident while on her way to fight the enemy in the Pacific. Had she been spared I feel sure she would have continued her fine work against the enemy in the best traditions of the French navy. Pray accept my deep sympathy.[12]

The *Thompson Lykes* was now in dry dock in New Orleans and the owners had wanted to take some photographs of the damage to her hull but were prevented from doing so by the US Navy. Why the Navy did this has never been explained. Eventually the Navy themselves produced two photographs.

Throughout these weeks no public announcement about the loss of *Surcouf* had been made, although on March 11 Mrs Warner had received a letter from the Royal Navy advising that her husband was missing presumed killed.[13] The letter asked her not to mention to anyone the name of the ship in which her husband had been serving so that knowledge of *Surcouf*'s loss would be denied to the enemy.

Mrs Gough, by then living in Dawlish, Devon, received a similar letter and with understandable bitterness recalls that it was followed by another twenty-four hours later peremptorily demanding the return of her allotment book (the amount of money her husband was sending her from his pay) which left her and her three children with nothing to live on. In an effort to sort things out Mrs Gough and her father travelled to Devonport where they saw the commandant. Much to her surprise, instead of sympathy and help over her money problems, she was roundly abused for coming and asking questions about her husband's death and told: 'It would be for my own good not to ask anything further and let things be.'[14]

It was to be several months before her pension finally began reaching her and, even then, the Admiralty insisted on deducting a day of her late husband's pay because they calculated he had died at 10.30 pm local time on February 18 and not 3.30 am London time on February 19.[15]

Roger's sister, Joan, had joined the Women's Royal Naval Service (WRNS) at the beginning of the war, and was commissioned as a Third Officer working in the cipher department at Devonport. By 1942, she had married and left the WRNS and, with a seventeen-month-old daughter, was living with her mother at Lamlash, on the Isle of Arran, off the west coast of Scotland.

In early March 1942, Mrs Burney received the usual letter of condolence from Buckingham Palace regretting the death of her son. However, as the letter did not say which son, Joan telephoned the Admiralty to find out if it referred to Christopher (serving with SOE) or Roger. Very reluctantly, the Admiralty admitted it was Roger, but told Joan to get off the line and ask no more questions.

Meanwhile Joan's husband, Lieutenant Commander Charles Adams, was serving as navigating officer in the cruiser HMS *Cardiff* and, when he heard of *Surcouf*'s loss, made enquiries as to the cause. He was told that *Surcouf* had been 'rammed by an American destroyer', but there was no suggestion this was anything other than an accident. The confusion of a destroyer instead of an American freighter was also not particularly significant. Commander Adams passed this information on to his wife by letter but, because these were subject to censorship, they had devised a private code so that, if he wrote the date on the letter in Portuguese (which he spoke fluently) then Joan knew every fifth word would be the coded message.

In this way Mrs Adams learned how her brother had died, but accepted it had been a cruel accident and, like Mme Blaison, it was not until many years after the war that she first heard rumours to the contrary. However, these three accounts do show the acute sensitivity then prevailing at the Admiralty about the loss of the British liaison crew in *Surcouf* which, inevitably, has helped fuel the rumours that the authorities had something to hide.

Pears was by then back in London and also heard the news. He wrote to his friend in Long Island, Mrs Mayer, on April 19:

We [Pears and Britten] have to register as pacifists which will take a little time. I hope very much that I shall be able to work with the Quakers. I think I shall join them. If only I were a better person. Last night there was the enclosed cutting in the paper. I'm dreadfully afraid it means Roger has gone. It is bitterly sad. It was such a vile job and such hideous company. Alas! alas! he was a sweet dear person.[16]

Due to a lack of liaison between Britain and America, on March 26 the US Navy announced that the *Thompson Lykes* had collided with an enemy submarine. Johnson was quoted as saying:[17]

The freighter crashed into the object head on with a heavy jolt and passed over it . . . the crew heard an explosion, presumably a torpedo, and some screams . . . two men were sighted in the water.

The following morning Lord Halifax sent a telegram to the Foreign Office:

Following for France Lib. Have denied categorically . . . the loss of *Surcouf*. Absolutely essential that nothing should be published on that matter.[18]

But the cat was out of the bag and – as so often happens – the more the British tried to deny the *Surcouf*'s loss the more rumours began to circulate and eventually on April 18 the BBC made a fleeting reference to its loss but gave no details. In Britain the news passed unnoticed because there were many more important things happening, including such events as the commando raid on the French port of St Nazaire, a threat to suppress the popular newspaper the *Daily Mirror* because of its criticism of the war effort, the award of the George Cross to the people of Malta, the capture of Bataan with 36,000 American prisoners, and the end of white bread.

American investigations into marine accidents involving merchant ships are conducted by the Bureau of Marine Inspection under the authority of the US Coast Guard and, at 10.30 am on March 11 1942, an inquiry commenced in secret in Room No. 313, at the Custom House in New Orleans.[19] The chairman of the inquiry was Harold B Finn, assistant US Attorney from Washington, assisted by Captain JL Ahern, of the US Coast Guard, and John F Oettl, a US Supervising Inspector, both from New Orleans. Commander RCS Garwood RN was authorized to be present and given permission to submit any questions he wished during the inquiry. No one from the Free French navy was allowed to attend.

The eleven witnesses called to give evidence were: Henry Johnson, master; Andrew Thompson, junior third mate; Arthur G Atwell, able seaman; Howard G Trim, able seaman; AB Cummiskey, chief engineer; Herman J Myers, US army gun crew; Dohrman Henke, US army gun crew; John L Brady, third assistant engineer; Ramon A Moraga, oiler; Joseph Marbutt, fireman; John E Fitzpatrick, seaman.

The inquiry was most professionally handled and the first witness, Johnson, described how he had been given his orders by the US Navy at Cristobal in the normal way to sail alone, not in a convoy, to Guantanamo Bay in Cuba, which was the return half of his voyage back to New Orleans. Johnson was to use a route and speed of his choice but had been told nothing about any other vessel in the area, friendly or unfriendly, whether merchant vessels or warships. As soon as it got dark all lights on the *Thompson Lykes* were extinguished as called for by the US Navy who were the charterers of the ship.

The inquiry accepted that at 9.30 pm Johnson had received a message from the US Navy at Cristobal ordering him to Cienfuegos instead of Guantanamo Bay which required a course change, but again he was given no warning of any vessels in the area.

When it came to the details of the collision, Johnson and Thompson agreed that the first they had seen of the other vessel was a small white flashing light appearing low to starboard. Thompson thought it might have been a powerful flashlight

153

being waved up and down. Atwell, Henke and Fitzpatrick also thought it was flashlight. It then reappeared dead ahead, meaning the other vessel was passing across their bows from right (starboard) to left (port). Twenty seconds later the two vessels collided.

Witnesses had different opinions about the severity of the impact. Johnson called it 'a running crash and the whole vessel was shaken and lights went out in my room [behind the bridge].' Thompson, asked if it was a wooden or steel vessel, said he thought it was steel. Trim, who was in the port passageway adjusting the blackout curtains, described it as not violent, did not even realize there had been a collision and thought it was 'an extra heavy wave' and 'just a few pickle jars in the mess room fell over.' Cummiskey was in his bunk and felt 'a fairly good jar' but not severe and said that it felt as if the ship 'was lifted out of the water'. Henke thought the ship 'just hesitated like hitting a heavy wave.' Brady was in the engine room and thought 'the ship had been torpedoed; it was quite a jolt with a sudden stop and then the forward motion that threw me across the guard rail. The stern of the ship came up and the [propeller] blade came out of the water . . . and the engine started to race, and then it fell back again.' Marbutt, also in the engine room, thought 'the ship had gone aground. It seemed to me it just went ashore – yes – slid on a beach . . . the ship rose forward . . . just a few seconds and then came down.' Fitzpatrick said it 'shook the ship'.

All the witnesses agreed there was a bright orange flash as the ships collided, followed by a dull explosion, another smaller flash, and then a smaller explosion that seemed to come from underwater alongside the ship. The explosion was felt more by those below in the engine room than those on deck or on the bridge.

As to the identity of the other vessel Johnson said it was 'very low in the water or partly submerged' causing him to tell the naval authorities in Cristobal that he had rammed an unidentified submarine. Thompson said immediately after the collision (his eyes being accustomed to dark unlike Johnson who had been in his office) that he saw something that he believed was the bow of a ship rise up out of the water on the port side and then disappear. He described it as 'long and narrow' and also thought it was a submarine. Myers said it was a 'black-looking bulk' but could not tell what sort of ship it was. Henke thought they had 'scraped a submarine and it went on the port side of us and was diving under us.' Fitzpatrick could not see the shape of the vessel but thought it sank by the port side. The Board did not ask how it was that on February 20 the naval authorities had been told the other vessel was possibly an armed launch.

Johnson could not say what sort of oil was on the water, nor did he try and take a sample, but mentioned the smell 'of hot diesel oil'. Thompson said he could smell 'burning oil'. Atwell said he smelled 'oil smoke, heavy oil smoke'. Trim saw an oil slick but it had come 'from our own ship' meaning the damaged forepeak tank. Myers and Henke thought it had the smell of crude oil.

Johnson heard cries for help and believed they were in English. So, too, did Trim who heard the word 'help' twice. Myers was closer and definitely heard the words in English 'help' and saw a man in what he described as a 'white sweatshirt with white sleeves'. Henke heard more than once voice calling 'help'. Fitzpatrick heard 'two fellows hollering out there to throw them down a rope [which no one had time to do], but they didn't say "rope" but "wope". That is why I think it was a foreign ship.'

At 11.05 am on March 13 the inquiry finished and the team of three went off to examine the *Thompson Lykes* in dry dock. On April 3 the board of inquiry submitted their findings to Rear Admiral RR Waesche, Commandant of the US Coast Guard in Washington.[20]

The Board . . . is satisfied that the collision was purely accidental and, so far as the . . . *Thompson Lykes* was concerned, unavoidable . . . the collision was caused by the operation of the two vessels on intersecting courses, without lights due to the exigencies of war.

155

Unfortunately, the testimony failed to disclose the identity of the lost vessel and, since there were no survivors, the Board is obliged to conclude that the *Thompson Lykes* collided with an unidentified vessel of unknown nationality . . . [and] . . . although her crew were convinced that they rammed an enemy submarine [because they had been given no information about any friendly submarine being in the area and therefore assumed any submarine must be hostile], there is nothing in the evidence to support that conclusion. The Board recommends . . . the investigation be closed without further action.

So far as can be determined from the transcript Commander Garwood asked no questions on behalf of the Admiralty.

In late June the US Navy sent a copy of the report to the Free French in Washington and the matter was then considered closed. In London, HA Smith, of DOD(F) at the Admiralty, wrote on June 27:

BAD Washington . . . is pointing out to the US Navy the failure to inform the *Thompson Lykes* of the route of the *Surcouf*, and it is considered that further representations in respect are unnecessary especially as *the onus for avoiding collision rested with Surcouf* [emphasis added]. It is noted that the general efficiency in *Surcouf* in regard to navigation and lookouts left much to be desired.[21]

A copy of the inquiry's report was also sent to the Admiralty and, on July 13 1942, GW Austin of the Military Branch, commented:

As far as M[ilitary] Branch is concerned there were no survivors from *Surcouf*. Presumably it is not intended that any action should be taken about the circumstances in which the vessel was lost, the awkwardness of which can be left to the Americans to explain.[22]

Two days later Captain EL Wharton wrote:

The loss of the *Surcouf* is presumably known to the
enemy; and the fact that there were no survivors makes
it all the more necessary that the true story of the fate of
so famous a French submarine should reach the relatives
of those who were lost. It would seem this is a matter
best handled by the US authorities . ... and now there is
a US naval public relations officer in London it should
not be difficult for [them] to co-ordinate with the fighting
French.[23]

At the beginning of August 1942 the Admiralty discovered that
the Free French naval headquarters in London had not received
a copy of the inquiry report and, naturally, were not only asking
for one, but also wanted to see the deck log of the *Thompson
Lykes*. On September 7 GW Austin, of M Branch at the
Admiralty, wrote:

It is considered as a general principle that the Admiralty
should not give the Free French any further information
without consultations with the Americans. C-in-C
A[merica] & W[est] I[ndies] . . . [*Malabar*] . . . did
inform the US authorities of *Surcouf*'s route and this
information was passed on to the commandant of the
15th naval district. It is not considered any further
request should be made for the deck log of the
Thompson Lykes. Sub-Lieutenant Burney's report is
quite unsuitable for transmission to the Free French.[24]

Two days later Captain GC Dickens RN added his views:

It is somewhat unfortunate that we ever mentioned the
existence of a report from the liaison officer on board
Surcouf. If we furnish Admiral Auboyneau [at the Free

French naval headquarters in London] with Sub-Lieutenant Burney's outspoken report, the feeling he probably holds that all liaison officers are somewhat in the nature of spies, will be strengthened. He may also feel that an unmerited slur has been cast upon his gallant officers and men. On the other hand if we refuse to meet his request he will at once assume that the report is an extremely adverse one and he may be more suspicious than ever about the sort of thing liaison officers tell us. Personally *I should lie wholeheartedly* [emphasis added] and say we cannot send the report as it was confined to personal matters to do with the BNLO himself and had no bearing on the accident.[25]

Dickens then proposed that the Free French be told that there did not appear any reason why *Surcouf* should have been escorted on the voyage from Bermuda to Panama; it was not practical to warn all ships of what other ships they might possibly meet, and that therefore there was no reason for having another inquiry into *Surcouf*'s loss.

On September 30 Horton added his comments:

Submarines are escorted *when in coastal waters* [original emphasis] to avoid incidents such as attacks by friendly aircraft or anti-submarine vessels . . . it is neither the practice to escort submarines *on the high seas* [original emphasis] nor to inform merchant vessels of the routes of our submarines . . . the onus of keeping clear always lies with the submarine. Even with these precautions there have been three collisions between British submarines and British merchant ships resulting in the loss of two of the submarines.[26]

The matter dragged on throughout October with the Free French becoming increasingly annoyed – and suspicious – by what they saw as deliberate stalling by the Admiralty and the Americans. The matter then lay quiet for several months until in

158

May 1943 (fifteen months after the disaster) Auboyneau suddenly raised the matter again this time by writing directly to Admiral Harold Stark USN, who was commander of US naval forces in London, asking that there should be a fresh inquiry into the loss of *Surcouf*. Stark passed Auboyneau's letter to his assistant, Commander Kitteridge USNR, who in turn asked the Admiralty for their views and wearily they reopened *Surcouf*'s bulky file.

The indefatigable GW Austin was soon hard at work and produced a long memorandum pointing out that Auboyneau had never said whether he agreed with the view that the collision was an accident or not, and whether he was objecting to the statement in the official report that the *Thompson Lykes* was not to blame, adding:

> This incidentally gives a further reason for not reopening the inquiry, as the question of attributing blame to somebody might be raised by the Free French representative.[27]

Austin's opinion went back to Kitteridge, thence to Stark, and eventually to Auboyneau but with the added agreement that at long last a copy of the *Thompson Lykes*' deck log would be made available to the Free French. Even then they had to wait until December 23 1943 before it was sent by the 8th Naval District in New Orleans, and all it consisted of was nine lines giving a brief description of the weather and the fact that they had collided with an unidentified craft which sank in about two minutes. The US Navy politely explained that all the other information the Free French had sought about whether the ship had been warned of *Surcouf*'s movements was not in the log.

The Free French realized they were neither going to be allowed a second inquiry, nor would any further information be forthcoming from either the British or Americans, and therefore they would have to be satisfied with the original official finding with which they plainly did not agree. Had the Free French been allowed to attend the official inquiry immediately after the loss, all the subsequent fuss and inevitable suspicions could have been avoided. Bearing in mind all the facts it is hard to see how the French could have brought a successful civil action against either the steamship company, or the US Navy who were chartering it, since clearly it was an accident caused by war.

The long delay in telling the next of kin in France what had happened to *Surcouf* not only soured relations with the Americans (who had never made any secret of their dislike for de Gaulle anyway) but also helped fuel bitterness and suspicion that created much of the mythology and rumour that still exists to this day.

NOTES

1. Folio 42, ADM 199/829 (PRO, Kew).
2. Seaworthy certificate 363-X, February 25 1942, issued by the American Bureau of Shipping, Record Group 041 (Civil Reference Branch, National Archives, Washington, DC).
3. Survey report No. 1460, February 25 1942, *ibid*.
4. Folio 42, ADM 199/829 (PRO, Kew).
5. Folio 44, *ibid*.
6. Folio 45, *ibid*.
7. Folios 40–1, *ibid*.
8. By JA Phillips, PAS(S).
9. Singapore surrendered on February 15 1942 to about 15,000 Japanese troops who had fought a brilliant campaign down the Malay peninsular that British experts had claimed was impenetrable.
10. Letter SM/28, Folio 49, ADM 199/829 (PRO, Kew); a copy is also in File TTY/683 (Vincennes Archives, Paris).
11. Letter No. 45913, QS15/EF28(420223), from Captain RE Schuirman USN to the Secretary of State, File 851.304/21 (National Archives, Washington, DC).
12. Vincennes Archives, Paris.
13. Warner papers kindly made available to the author by Mr and Mrs Stanley Warner.
14. Interview with Mrs LE Cook (previously Mrs Gough) at Bexhill on Sea, August 1 1990. The author is greatly indebted to Mrs Cook and her daughter, Mrs Valerie Buckle, for their help in making available all Bernard Gough's naval papers and personal records.
15. Letter dated October 13 1942, from commodore RN barracks, Portsmouth. Mrs Warner received a similar letter.
16. *Letters From A Life: The Selected Letters and Diaries of Benjamin Britten:*

1913–1976, edited by Dr Donald Mitchell & Dr Phillip Reed (Faber, 1991). The author is most grateful for being allowed to quote from the advance proofs of this book.

17. By Associated Press in New Orleans and reported in the *Evening Star*, Washington, March 27 1942, '*Enemy Sub Rammed and Sunk by US Vessel in Caribbean*'.
18. Message No. 1829, Z2660/317/17, Folio 51, ADM 199/829 (PRO, Kew).
19. Record Group 041 (Civil Reference Branch, National Archives, Washington, DC).
20. File 851.304/21 (National Archives, Washington, DC).
21. Folio 53, ADM 199/829 (PRO, Kew).
22. *Ibid.*
23. *Ibid.*
24. Folio 54, *ibid.*
25. *Ibid.*
26. Folio 55, *ibid.*
27. Folios 56–7, *ibid.*

CHAPTER 9
MYTHS AND RUMOURS

It has always been claimed that the rumours that *Surcouf* had been deliberately sunk by the Americans, or the British, was part of some ingenious propaganda campaign created by a combination of German and Vichy French intelligence. This is untrue. Had the Germans wanted to capitalize on *Surcouf*'s loss then their first most obvious target would have been Mme Blaison because she was living with her brother-in-law who was, to put it mildly, on good terms with the Germans. It would have been very easy for the Germans, via the Vichy government, to have made much out of rendering their condolences, and then quietly to have leaked stories that *Surcouf*'s loss was not quite what it seemed, and that it had, in fact, been sunk by the British who had accused its loyal crew of treachery.

Presented in the right way such a story would have found many ready ears in France, perhaps even those of Mme Blaison. But nothing of the sort every happened. Mme Blaison learned of her husband's death around April 1942, but it was not until the mid 1960s that anyone suggested to her that there was something mysterious about the loss of *Surcouf*, or that it might have been deliberately sunk by the Americans.[1]

With the benefit of hindsight one has to remember that in wartime service personnel often spend long periods in isolated situations with nothing to do but grumble and gossip. Indeed, it would be a sign that something was seriously wrong if service-men did not do this. In the Royal Navy there is a great tradition of what is called 'buzz': news which circulates around the lower deck largely prompted by wishful thinking and a few scraps of information obtained by those who may have overheard some conversation between officers. As gossip is passed from one to another so it is magnified both in order to impress the listener and to suit his preconceived beliefs. Another problem with war-time gossip is that, for obvious reasons of security, there cannot be any public access to official records to check the facts, nor can any inquiries be publicly held.

In 1941 the French were not popular in the eyes of the average British serviceman. The view propagated by the heavily cen-sored newspaper reports and newsreels depicted the BEF as having fought bravely against overwhelming odds. The Belgians were seen to be surrendering on one side, and the French only too anxious to make peace on the other, thus British troops were forced to carry out the brilliantly executed evacuation at Dunkirk. A widely held view was that it was far better for Britain and the Commonwealth to be on their than have unreli-able allies like France who collapsed at the first sign of fighting.[2] It was, therefore, not surprising that the general reaction to all foreigners – even those who had come to Britain to continue the fight against Hitler – was one of distrust. Add to all this that it was only *Surcouf* which had been involved in a shoot-out when taken over in 1940 (resulting in the deaths of three British sailors) and it is not hard to see why anything unpleasant about the vessel – however ridiculous – would be believed.

The first rumour about *Surcouf*'s behaviour started in April 1941, when she was escorting eastbound convoy HX-118 and was suddenly detached and ordered back to Devonport. When the convoy reached Britain, stories circulated that *Surcouf* had tor-pedoed some of the ships in the convoy. As has been explained in Chapter 5, all this is absurd. The plan to recall *Surcouf* back to Devonport and convert her into a cargo-carrying submarine to take supplies to Malta had been agreed before the convoy sailed. What had upset the crews of the merchant ships was the

163

sudden and unexpected sight of a large, strange submarine appearing fleetingly out of the murk. No one had been warned that a submarine would form part of the escort and, not surprisingly, to merchant seamen all submarines in such circumstances were attacking.

The next rumour which circulated about *Surcouf* was that its crew were disloyal and planned to mutiny, take over the ship, and either go back to France or Martinique. Here there is some truth. Martin had been reluctant to bring *Surcouf* to Britain in the first place and would have preferred to go to Oran and join the rest of the French fleet.[3] The only reason he stayed was because the vessel was in a state of disrepair and could not sail. The crew recruited after the takeover had no interest in fighting for anyone and only wanted to go back to France.

All the BNLOs recognized this and mentioned it repeatedly in their reports to Horton which were considered so sensitive that none was ever shown to the French. In contrast both Ortoli and Blaison glossed over these problems and always reported the morale of their crew in glowing terms, as did Muselier when he visited *Surcouf* in Halifax on December 13 1941: he claimed he had never seen a submarine so well kept and immaculate and conveniently forgot that she had only just completed an $800,000 refit.

Before dealing with the rumours surrounding the loss of *Surcouf* there are two other bizarre stories that need airing. The first of these concerns Bernard Gough who it is alleged sent a radio message from *Surcouf* to *Malabar* some time after leaving Bermuda on February 12 saying: 'I am locked in the wireless room, this is it. I've got a revolver. Look after the wife and children.'[4]

This message was alleged to have been seen by Leslie Waldron who not only happened to be Gough's brother-in-law, but was also a master-at-arms (senior petty officer) in the Royal Navy stationed at *Malabar*. The story would appear to fit exactly the scenario that might have occurred had *Surcouf*'s crew decided to mutiny and defect. But is it true?

For a start the text is far more dramatic than one would expect an experienced telegraphist to send in an emergency and much more like something from a Hollywood film. The whole purpose of naval communications training is to eliminate unclear messages in times of stress. What, for example, does 'this is it' mean? Why bother to tell *Malabar* he has a revolver? If we are to assume that *Surcouf*'s crew had mutinied, and Gough was the only one of the liaison team who managed to reach the radio room, then one would expect him to send something like:

> Most urgent. Crew mutinied. Captain and first officer
> dead. Unsure whereabouts BNLO. Position
> approximately XXXX. Am destroying CBs [confidential
> books]. Urgent help needed.

Gough would also have continued transmitting for as long as possible so that *Malabar* and other shore stations could obtain a fix on *Surcouf*'s position.

Gough's message cannot be found in any archive, nor is there any reference to it in the war diary for *Malabar*. But how did a master-at-arms at *Malabar* come to see this message? The simple answer is that he could not have seen it because Waldron's service record[5] shows he was not at *Malabar* at the time. Waldron, who died in 1988, always refused to elaborate on his story, or provide any evidence, because he claimed if he did so the Navy would take away his pension.[6]

Waldron also claimed that when he met his brother-in-law who was on leave visiting New York in September 1941 (while *Surcouf* was under repair) Gough told him that conditions on board were so bad, and the crew so unreliable, that he 'felt sure he would not be alive long'.

The second story is even stranger and concerns Warner and Gough.[7] The tale begins when Lawrence Stannard and John Green left *Surcouf* at Halifax on January 15 1942 (after their brief stay on board) and then sailed in HMCS *Cowisham* to the US Navy yard at Philadelphia, on the Delaware River, to rejoin the submarine *L-27* which was still undergoing a refit. Some time later a signalman, Brian 'Spud' Murphy, with the submarine HMS *Parthian* (then refitting at the US Navy yard at Portsmouth), was injured in an accident while on leave in New York and Stannard was sent to replace him.

Parthian completed its refit and in late February 1942 sailed for the Mediterranean, but some days out into the Atlantic (in an accident identical to one that had happened to *Surcouf* on July 18 1941) submerged with the conning tower hatch still open and started to flood. Although too modest to admit it, the official record shows that Stannard was instrumental in saving the vessel which managed to resurface. It struggled back to Bermuda but, because of the extensive damage to the batteries and switchgear, had to return to the US Navy yard at Portsmouth, New Hampshire, for repairs.

The gunlayer in *Parthian* was Leonard Charles Oates, then aged twenty-one, who had joined submarines on May 12 1941. During *Parthian*'s earlier refit at Portsmouth, Oates had met seventeen-year-old Natalie Christine Bonnell who lived with her parents Walter and Elsie in Worcester, Massachusetts.[8] The couple evidently decided to take advantage of *Parthian*'s unexpected return to Portsmouth and, on March 28 1942, before the Rev Clinton L Morrill, Natalie and Leonard were married at Dover some twenty miles north of Portsmouth.

By this time the loss of *Surcouf* was public knowledge, although no details had been given. After a short honeymoon, Oates returned to *Parthian* which was still at Portsmouth and, in the course of conversation with his colleagues, asked if anyone knew a couple of sailors called Gough and Warner. Stannard replied that he had known them and that it was a tragedy they had been lost in *Surcouf*. 'They're not lost in *Surcouf*', replied Oates, 'Natalie and I met them in a bar the other day in Boston. They were with two women and are going to start a new life somewhere in the States.'

Parthian eventually completed its refit and sailed for the Mediterranean but, some time later, Oates transferred to HMS *Turbulent* and lost his life when it was sunk on March 23 1943. Natalie Oates continued to live at 12, Mattson Avenue, Worcester, working as an assembler at the nearby Raytheon Company until, on October 10 1946, she married Hugh F Bibb and went to live with him in South Carolina where she died in 1985 aged sixty-four.

This story has appeared in other forms: one version is that Gough and Warner were seen drinking in a bar in New York. The fundamental point, however, is the same: the pair had deserted *Surcouf* before she sailed from Bermuda presumably because they believed the crew would mutiny. Can the tale be true?

If it is, then the story about Gough's last radio message cannot be because he was not in *Surcouf* to make it. It also grotesquely implies that both of them would suddenly abandon their wives which, if one reads Warner's affectionate last letter to his written on February 11,[9] is quite impossible to contemplate. Lastly, desertion in wartime is an extremely serious offence and not one that two ratings with a long history of loyalty and impeccable service in the Royal Navy would even consider, however distasteful their posting.

There are several other flaws in the story. First, we know from Rose Baker that the pair said goodbye to her on the morning of February 12 so, even if they had nothing to smile about, the decision to desert must have been taken between then and 3 pm that same afternoon. Second, if the pair had failed to report on board *Surcouf*, Burney would have had to signal to *Malabar* that they were absent without leave. In a small place like Bermuda it would not have taken long to find them and, even if *Surcouf* sailed without them, there would be a record of the affair. Third, without any great resources how would the pair have got off Bermuda and back to America in wartime?

The only outstanding question – that cannot now be answered – is why Oates mentioned the names of Gough and Warner when he had never met them before and did not know they had been in *Surcouf*? The most plausible answer is that Oates and his wife never actually met them, but were retelling someone else's piece of gossip as a fact. In any case, if Gough and Warner were on the run from the Navy, why identify themselves to another naval rating who might well have gone straight to the local police? The whole tale is both absurd and rude to the memories of two very brave men. It also shows, however, what bizarre tales surround *Surcouf*.

The fate of the liaison team turns up in another account, supposedly from an American ex-sailor who, in 1942, was serving in a submarine in the north Atlantic.[10] While on submerged patrol they saw *Surcouf* on the surface and, through their periscope, watched as her crew threw three large objects into the water. After she had disappeared, the American submarine surfaced and found the bodies of three men which it was assumed were Burney, Gough and Warner. The same source also claims that an ex-Royal Canadian naval officer, serving at *Malabar* in 1942, recalled seeing a signal from an American submarine reporting this incident. As one would expect, neither the American nor the Canadian has ever been identified nor of course is there any record of such an incident in any American submarine log book or in *Malabar*'s war diary. Furthermore, if the three bodies had been recovered there would have been the matter of their burial.

The stock answer for the lack of written records for this and similar incidents is that they would not have been entered because of official policy to conceal the affair. This stands logic on its head by arguing that because there is no mention of it in the records it must be true. Laughable though this may sound there is some merit to the argument. Other sensitive wartime issues have been deliberately concealed, so at this point it is worth briefly digressing to consider an excellent example – the Ultra secret concerning the breaking of German *Enigma* codes.

The Ultra story remained a secret long after the war, not to hide it from the Russians, who knew all about it anyway, but for the pragmatic reason that Britain was busy selling reconditioned *Enigma*s to Third World countries. They assured them it would provide top-grade security whereas, in fact, it enabled Britain and America to read all their communications for the next twenty years to devastating effect. By the late 1960s the story was beginning to emerge in articles and books in Poland and France, with the result that in 1974 the government reluctantly sanctioned publication of a sanitized version,[11] and also released some Ultra summaries (but not the original intercepts) into the Public Record Office.

This example not only shows how very important matters can be concealed, but also how difficult it is for anyone to discover the truth if no records are available. In 1959, the very experienced defence correspondent of the *Daily Express*, Chapman Pincher, was given a strong hint that Britain had been reading German codes during the war.[12] But, because he could find no documentary evidence, and none of those who knew about the Ultra story would talk to him, Pincher concluded the story was untrue. Had he attempted to make such a claim without any proof it would have sounded as ridiculous as claiming that *Surcouf* was deliberately sunk by the allies.

Under the circumstances it would be unwise to assume that all the secrets of World War II have been exposed[13] and, with this thought in mind, we can now consider the likelihood of the various claims that *Surcouf* was deliberately destroyed by the Americans and British. There are certainly no lack of accounts as to how this was achieved.

At the outset there is one extremely important point to consider. *Surcouf* was a very large submarine and, for reasons already explained, spent most of its last weeks travelling only on the surface. When a submarine is destroyed underwater, whether by depth charges or an internal accident, it is rare to have survivors although, on some occasions, the stricken vessel does manage to come to the surface allowing a few members of the crew to escape before its final plunge. If, however, a submarine is attacked on the surface the chance of survivors is much greater. There will usually be several crew on the bridge in the conning tower, and others nearby in the control room, who will have an opportunity to jump overboard and survive. This would present the attackers with a problem for there is not a western sailor who would not rescue other sailors from a sinking ship and, if they simply abandoned them, there is no reason why they might not be found by some other vessel.

The first rumours that *Surcouf* had been attacking allied ship-

169

ping and had been sunk by either the British or Americans began in Bermuda and had nothing to do with German intelligence. On April 18 1942, Kennedy-Purvis told the Admiralty:

> The BBC statement announcing the loss of *Surcouf* has been received in Bermuda today, but on account of its brevity it has done little to allay the rumours . . . that *Surcouf* was operating against allied shipping, in fact [they] appear to have gained strength. After consultation with the governor, I have issued a statement . . . to the effect that *Surcouf* was lost in the course of normal war duties . . . and any rumours to the contrary are malicious inventions.[14]

Bermuda certainly was – and remains to this day – a hotbed of gossip about *Surcouf*. One group of unidentified Bermudians claim to have hunted her in a naval vessel after she started shelling allied merchant shipping.

Graham Copeland who, in 1942, was a chief petty officer in the supply department at *Malabar*, recalls that convoys bound for Europe gathered off St George's before starting out across the Atlantic.[15] Stories began to circulate that every time *Surcouf* left Bermuda on patrol, ships would be lost in the convoy, and she was said to have torpedoed them. As with so many *Surcouf* tales there can be no truth in it for the simple reason that it would have been impossible for her to fire her torpedoes or 8-inch guns without the BNLO knowing and, furthermore, there were no replacement stocks of either in Bermuda. Had suspicions of this nature seriously existed amongst the authorities it would have been very easy to have checked the stocks of munitions on board *Surcouf* before and after each patrol, and Burney makes no mention of this ever happening in his reports.

The next story begins with two American submarines – USS *L-16* and USS *L-18* – that are said to have arrived 'unexpectedly' in Bermuda on February 4 1942, and then left on February 9 having been 'mysteriously placed under the control of British naval intelligence in Jamaica'.[16] The purpose of their mission was to lie in wait for *Surcouf* when she made a dash for the safety of Martinique and then sink her. The only problem with this account is that the US Navy's *L-Class* submarines were decommissioned and sold for scrap in the 1920s, the last of that class, *L-9*, being scrapped in 1923.[17] Furthermore, the highest number that class went was *L-11*.

Another story concerns the British cruiser HMS *Diamede* which is said to have left *Malabar* in great haste a few days after *Surcouf* had sailed.[18] When *Diamede* returned, her crew boasted to Bermudians that they had caught *Surcouf* on the surface and sunk her by gunfire. The morning after the sinking it is alleged that the captain read a signal from Kennedy-Purvis in Bermuda ordering them not to mention the episode. All one can say about this is that no evidence exists to prove or disprove it, but it is surely remarkable that for fifty years not a soul on board has ever ignored this order and commented on what must have been a remarkable event.

But yet another story, which has enjoyed remarkable circulation, claims that *Surcouf* was never anywhere near Martinique but had gone north after leaving Bermuda and, on February 20, attempted to torpedo the 80,000-ton liner RMS *Queen Mary* as it left Boston harbour crammed with American troops bound for Britain.[19] Not content with that, *Surcouf* then met up with a German *U-boat* off Long Island and, while refuelling her, was spotted by the American submarine USS *Marlin* who sank her.

The latter story first appeared in 1964:[20] an American diver, Mr Lee Prettyman Jr, of Hartford, Connecticut, claimed to have been told it by a US Navy petty officer (who he refused to identify 'in case he got into trouble with his superiors') he met in Newport while Prettyman and his salvage team were diving on the wreck of the *U-853* in Block Island Sound off Long Island. The *U-853* was sunk on May 6 1945 by the USS *Atherton* and the USS *Mobile*.

The next day Prettyman took this petty officer out in his salvage vessel and, with the aid of sonar, found a wreck about 400-feet long lying in around 130 feet of water. When Prettyman

171

dived on it he found it was *Surcouf*:

> *Surcouf* leans to port, lying in sand, rocks, and mud. I
> couldn't believe the size of it. With this hangar that looks
> like a boiler on it, it was a ship on top of a ship. It was a
> weird experience swimming alongside it . . . it seemed
> never to end. I could tell it was the *Surcouf* by that
> hangar and that fat conning tower. I went along until I
> came to a hole about 25 feet long and 10 feet high
> blasted in the hull forward of the conning tower.

Prettyman later claimed he had made several other dives on this
wreck and salvaged one of the two propellers (which he incorrectly states was made of copper) but immediately sold it for
scrap to someone he refused to name, and recovered other
pieces of scrap which he was also unable to produce.

It is certainly an intriguing tale graphically told (as is often the
case with wreck claims) but, bearing in mind the profit potential
if it was indeed the wreck of *Surcouf*, one wonders why Prettyman did not at least photograph it. In fact, no more was ever
heard of Prettyman and, according to the US Navy, the only
submarine wreck known to be in the area were the remains of
the USS *Bass* deliberately sunk by the US Navy during torpedo
tests in February 1945.[21]

Another version of this tale appeared in the autumn 1990
issued of *The Review*, a quarterly journal dealing with naval
history and research. In this, Colin Burrow of Leeds wrote that:

> Shortly after dark on 18th February [1942] an American
> destroyer on patrol in the approaches to the Panama
> Canal fired a starshell over an unidentified vessel. There
> were, in fact, two vessels in the light of the flares, one
> was a Type VII or IX *U-boat*, the other was *Surcouf* and
> she was refuelling and rearming the German vessel. The
> American vessel . . . immediately opened fire . . . hits
> were recorded on both submarines but, after dropping a
> full, standard depth charge pattern, the destroyer

captain, obeying the old edict 'discretion is the better part of valour', broke off the attack.

Apparently Mr Burrow got his story from a retired member of the US Navy who, as with similar claims, was unable to provide any evidence to substantiate it. Aside from the elementary question of how *Surcouf* managed to contact and rendezvous with a German *U-boat*, it is impossible to believe that a destroyer captain with two enemy submarines in front of him and already hit, would have retired from the scene. It is also implausible that, after a naval career of such staggering inefficiency, in her death throes *Surcouf* should have acquired such incredible strategic prowess and be able to refuel a German submarine at sea for which it possessed no equipment.

A further tale claims that on March 3 1942 the Canadian destroyer HMCS *Annapolis* detached herself from a convoy near Cape Race, Newfoundland, to go to the aid of a large Polish destroyer which was apparently attacking a submarine.[22] The name of this destroyer is not known, but one suggestion is that it was the *Piorun* (conveniently the same ship that reported *Surcouf* attacking merchant vessels in Convoy HX 118 in April 1941). It is alleged that the Polish destroyer told *Annapolis* that she had just sunk *Surcouf* 'after finding her in the company of a German *U-boat*', and asked the Canadian ship to report the sinking verbally to naval authorities when they returned to Halifax thus preserving radio silence. Meantime, the crew of *Annapolis* were instructed to say nothing about the matter and none has for fifty years.

As with the earlier story of HMS *Diamede*, this tale cannot be proved one way or the other (although both De Wolff and Audette, who were in senior positions with the RCN at Halifax at the time, consider it ridiculous) but if it were true then a large number of people would know about the incident and it seems remarkable that not one has ever spoken out in all these years.

The first direct French involvement in these stories came to light on June 18 1942 when Lieutenant FP Holcomb USMCR, an assistant naval attaché at the American consulate in Tangier, forwarded an intelligence report to the Navy Department in Washington in which he described a meeting between the vice-consul in Casablanca and Mme Drogou who was the widow of the captain of the Free French submarine *Narval*, which had been lost in the Mediterranean in December 1940.[23]

Apparently, in 1941, Mme Drogou had told the American consul in Casablanca that there had been reports that her husband and his crew had been attempting to defect from the Free French and return to France, whereupon the British sent two vessels after the *Narval* and sank her. The consul had passed this on to the American Embassy in London on October 1 1941 who, in turn, told Muselier and eventually a reply came back to Casablanca from his headquarters saying they were satisfied *Narval* had been sunk through enemy action.

Now Mme Drogou was back again, this time to tell the consul a similar story about *Surcouf*:

> That the French navy had circulated a rumour that *Surcouf* had been sunk by gunfire by an American cruiser in the north Atlantic. She stated that a friend of hers had gone to the [French] Admiralty in Casablanca and there had been shown a paper in which it was stated definitely that the American Navy admitted sinking *Surcouf* under these circumstances . . . *Surcouf* had been resting on the surface when the American cruiser sighted it and sank it without warning. This information has had a disturbing affect [sic] on de Gaullist and pro-American French in Casablanca. [The] consulate has learned that certain officers of the local navy are circulating rumours . . . that *Surcouf* was deliberately sunk because 'its crew were not considered loyal or reliable by the Americans'. Mme Drogou has been in touch with a number of French-women in Casablanca . . . and two women in France, whose husbands were known to have been on the *Surcouf* . . . these women have made enquiries about their husbands but can get no information.

Holcomb's report reached the Admiralty on July 9 1942, where the Military Branch commented it was a matter for the Americans to explain the 'awkwardness' of *Surcouf*'s disappearance and they had no intention of getting involved.[24] However, Captain EL Wharton RN wrote that for the sake of good relations with the French, 'of all ways of thinking', it would be better to have a complete exposure of all the circumstances surrounding the loss of *Surcouf*:

> There is, I believe, every reason to suppose that she was sunk at night in collision with a US merchant ship in the Caribbean, though this can only be deduced from circumstances of loss.

Despite Wharton's suggestion being approved, nothing was done about it until late 1943, apparently because the Admiralty were reluctant to upset the Americans. The excuse for this was that if the French were told too much about the collision they might try and bring a civil action against the Lykes Steamship Company but, set against the damage these rumours were doing to French morale in the middle of a world war, this seems remarkably unconvincing. For those seeking a more sinister reason this reluctance could be interpreted as meaning the Admiralty knew perfectly well that the Americans had indeed deliberately sunk the vessel.

As a result rumours continued to circulate reaching an ever wider audience so that, on May 25 1942, Miss Pauline A Azbell, of 3, Prospect Street, New London, Connecticut, wrote to Lieutenant Colonel R Brunschwig, at the Free French Delegation at 626, Fifth Avenue, New York, that she had heard stories both locally, and from Halifax and Bermuda, that *Surcouf* had been sunk by a British warship because its crew had become pro-Nazi. The head of the Free French mission, Colonel PG de Chevigne, sent Miss Azbell's letter on to Colonel Henry Cunningham, at the War Department in Washington, adding:

> It is very likely that this rumour was put into circulation by a person having a disordered imagination or it may be

175

the fruit of thoughtless babbling. While in Syria I was responsible for the [French] security service and had in my possession a copy of German espionage instructions to its agent . . . [which] . . . was to divide English and French and to embitter any existing disunity.[25]

Fanciful stories about *Surcouf*'s demise continued and included the claim that an aircraft from No. 202 Squadron RAF Coastal Command, operating out of Gibraltar, had sunk her off north Africa, and another that *Surcouf* had been shadowed during her voyage to Panama and deliberately rammed and sunk. The former story is not confirmed by the squadron's very detailed records, and, as to the latter, deliberately sinking a 3000-ton submarine by ramming can be as hazardous to the surface craft as to the intended victim and there are plenty of instances during the war where both sank.

One intriguing story, that is not so easy to dismiss casually, comes from John Booth who, in 1946, was a signalman attached to HMS *Malabar*. According to the transcript of a conversation between Mr Booth and the archivist at the RN Submarine Museum on September 9 1987, Mr Booth said:

> That while on the C-in-C West Indies staff at *Malabar*, in
> 1946, he went back through the confidential files and
> claims he saw signals between the Admiralty and
> *Malabar* about the liaison team in *Surcouf*. These said
> that the liaison team should not be taken off at Bermuda
> because, if this was done, the French might suspect
> something untoward was going on. Mr Booth went on to
> say that the Admiralty signals he saw specifically
> mentioned there was to be an attack on *Surcouf* after she
> had left Bermuda for Tahiti. Mr Booth insisted that
> *Surcouf* had been sunk deliberately.[26]

The first part of this story is certainly true. As described in Chapter 6, there was a flurry of messages in February 1942 between London and Bermuda about the future of the liaison

team. Unfortunately, no records of the other messages Mr
Booth mentions exist – either in Bermuda or London – thus the
final proof is once again elusive. Inevitably one wonders why
such sensitive signals would have remained in files accessible to
ordinary naval personnel many years after the event but, nevertheless, Mr Booth is quite adamant that he saw them.

A final twist to the story is to be found in the archives at the
Naval Historical Branch in London, where *Surcouf*'s career
from 1940 onwards is recorded on nine index cards. Eight of
these are headed: 'French (Free) *Surcouf*', but the ninth and
final card is headed: 'French (Vichy) *Surcouf*'. Though it would
be unwise to place too much importance on one index card written up after the war from the Admiralty's war diary, it must
raise the question of why such a controversial change in the
heading was made, bearing in mind that the Admiralty had
always assured the Free French that they accepted claims that
Surcouf had changed sides were totally false.

A more complex and important tale involved the late Sir
William Stephenson who, as previously mentioned, ran MI6's
operations in New York during the war. Although many colourful, and sometimes inaccurate stories, have been written about
Stephenson, the basic facts are that before the war he was a
wealthy, and very patriotic, Canadian businessman who,
because of his extensive knowledge of European trade, became
involved in espionage through the Industrial Intelligence Centre
in London headed by Churchill's friend, Desmond Morton.

Even before he became prime minister in 1940, Churchill had
always maintained close links with a number of wealthy individ-
uals who provided him, sometimes through Morton, scraps of
intelligence about the Germans. Stephenson's entrepreneurial
spirit appealed to Churchill's love of adventure and intrigue
(another of his private agents was Alexander Korda, the controversial film-maker) and in June 1940 he sent Stephenson to
New York.

After the war, Sir William Stephenson retired to Bermuda
and, in the mid 1980s, was asked by Kevin Stevenson, assistant
editor of the *Royal Gazette*, about the *Surcouf* affair.[27] Steven-

son knew Sir William well and frequently talked with him because Stevenson's father, confusingly William Stevenson, had written the biography about Sir William entitled *A Man Called Intrepid*.[28]

Without any hesitation, Sir William told Kevin Stevenson that after the St Pierre and Miquelon affair in late 1941, he was asked by Churchill to decide whether *Surcouf*'s crew could be relied on. Sir William concluded they could not and, therefore, was ordered by Churchill to destroy her. To achieve this, Stephenson engaged the services of two people in Bermuda, Guy Ridgeway and Hamish Mitchell, who were to arrange for limpet mines to be attached to *Surcouf*'s hull before she sailed on February 12, timed to explode the following day when she would be at least 300 miles away in deep water.

Sir William had never mentioned this story previously, nor has it ever been mentioned in any of the books written about him, and it is also true that, following a heart attack, Sir William's memory sometimes failed him. However, Kevin Stevenson recalls the statement was made with complete clarity and without any hesitation, and certainly had all the hallmarks of truth about it.

What makes the story particularly intriguing is that both those named existed and were closely involved with Sir William and BSC. As we have seen, Ridgeway was in charge of naval intelligence at *Malabar* and had already interrogated *Surcouf*'s crew and concluded more than half were pro-Vichy so it is logical to assume that Sir William would have been guided by what Ridgeway told him.

Hamish Mitchell was born in Fife, Scotland, in 1899 and in 1930 married Elsa Mott, the daughter of Charles Stewart Mott, one of the largest shareholders in the General Motors Corporation. From 1931 to 1937 the Mitchells lived in London, and then came out to Bermuda and bought a large property called Heron's Nest, which the family still owns. Apart from 'managing a large portfolio of shares', Mitchell apparently did no other work although he seems to have had a connection with Bermuda Industrial Gases. Mr Walter Seymour, who worked for Mitchell

for more than twenty-five years, described him as: 'Very tough
. . . a man of action . . . very patriotic and someone who would
serve England at any time.'[29]

It would not be unreasonable to suggest that, even before
1939, Mitchell was another of Churchill's private spies. After the
war began, Mitchell went to work in the Lend-Lease office in
New York then returning to work at the censorship section at
the Princess Hotel. According to his only daughter, Joan (now
Mrs Joan McGillary), her father actually worked directly for Sir
William. Much of his work was very mysterious; she recalled
how he made many secret trips away from Bermuda, and that
Sir William used to stay regularly at Heron's Nest during the
war.[30]

After the war Admiral De Wolff, who had been involved with
Surcouf during its visit to Halifax, also retired to Bermuda and
during the 1960s became a close friend of Sir William. He, too,
discussed the *Surcouf* affair with Sir William and, although he
would not be drawn into specific details, De Wolff got the clear
impression that Sir William had been involved with its destruction. De Wolff also heard about the story of the limpet mines.

If Sir William's story is true, then he could not have chosen a
better pair to carry out his instructions. Mitchell was plainly the
sort of man who would do anything he believed to be in Britain's
interests, and destroying a rogue French submarine would not
give him cause for concern. Ridgeway already believed *Surcouf*'s crew were unreliable, knew all about the exchange of
messages with London and when *Surcouf* would sail, and could
easily have obtained two limpet mines and the divers to fix them
to the hull.

What might have happened next is unclear. One version is
that the crew discovered the mines and, realizing the British
were prepared to kill them, decided to make a run for Martinique. Somewhere off St Pierre, Martinique, on March 3 1942
they were intercepted and sunk, and Sir William is then said to
have written to J Edgar Hoover, head of the Federal Bureau of
Investigation (FBI), and told him this. In turn, on March 12,
Hoover wrote to Rear Admiral TS Wilkinson USN, director of

179

the Office of Naval Intelligence in Washington: 'Information has been received from a highly confidential source that the French submarine *Surcouf* was sunk off St Pierre on March 3 1942.'

From the only known reproduction of this letter it appears genuine,[31] but the whereabouts of the original is a mystery. The FBI prides itself on its voluminous and meticulously kept archives (especially those relating to Hoover's own correspondence), yet when the author asked to see the file in which this letter was kept he was told:

> We were not able to locate . . . a J Edgar Hoover letter dated March 12 1942 to Rear Admiral TS Wilkinson. Furthermore our records indicate that this document was not located or retrieved pursuant to previous Freedom of Information Act requests.[32]

The final comment is particularly strange because it implies the reproduction did not come from FBI archives but presumably from naval intelligence records. In 1986 a copy of this letter could be found in the *Surcouf* file in the Vincennes Archives but that, too, has since disappeared. Disappearing documents are a nightmare to the historian but a godsend to those wishing to create mysteries.

What is strange is why Sir William would have wanted to have told anyone – especially Hoover – anything about *Surcouf* if he had arranged its destruction. The guiding rule for such covert operations is the less that appears in writing the better. Far better for *Surcouf* to disappear and let others create the mystery.

Experience with intelligence matters shows that the more bizarre the claim, the more likely it is to be true. Nevertheless, with no other evidence forthcoming, and all the participants dead, it would be wise to consider two possibilities: first, the proposal to destroy *Surcouf* was no more than a contingency plan unofficially discussed by Sir William with Ridgeway and Mitchell, but never carried out. Second, the limpet mines were placed on the hull but were discovered by the crew after leaving

Bermuda, thus convincing Blaison he could not trust either the British or the Americans, so he decided to make a run for Martinique.

What is clear from this incredible range of stories is that the Germans played no part in circulating them, and by 1942 showed no interest in *Surcouf* or the rest of the Free French navy. All the rumours about *Surcouf* came from British and American sources and needed no help from the enemy. Thus only *Surcouf* generated this amazing mythology almost all of which was untrue and the product of evil and wishful thinking. Yet there are just sufficient unexplained incidents to take the story beyond the usual cock-up theory and into the realms of a conspiracy. With these in mind, we can now turn to the final hours of *Surcouf*.

NOTES

1. Blaison interview.
2. In 1940, King George VI wrote to his mother Queen Mary, 'I feel happier now we have no allies to be polite to and to pamper', while a Hampstead reader wrote to the magazine *Picture Post*, 'A nation without allies is a nation with no one to let them down'.
3. Martin's report, ref: 30063/EM (Vincennes Archives, Paris).
4. *Who Killed Surcouf?, op. cit.*, 49.
5. Private information from Ministry of Defence source to the author.
6. Mrs Cook interview, August 1990.
7. Stannard interview.
8. The author is most grateful to David J Rushford, Assistant City Clerk, at Worcester, Mass, for his help in tracing the marriage certificates and other details of Mr and Mrs Oates. The author was also greatly helped by David Lawler of the Worcester *Telegram & Gazette* in tracing the family background of Natalie Bonnell.
9. Warner private archives.
10. *Who Killed Surcouf?, op. cit.*, 64.
11. *The Ultra Secret*, Fred Winterbotham (Weidenfeld & Nicholson, 1974). It was not Winterbotham's fault that his book contained so many errors: he had nothing to do with the breaking of the *Enigma*, but was only responsible for disseminating the information obtained from the decrypts. As a result Winterbotham's account was based on what he remembered and completely ignored the pre-war contribution of Polish and French codebreakers which caused great offence.
12. *Inside Story*, Chapman Pincher (Sidgwick & Jackson, 1978), 220–1.

13. Claims persistently surface that Churchill operated a small group of agents whom he personally sent into occupied France to carry out assassinations and other covert operations. One such account is *Churchill's Secret Agent*, Josephine Butler (Blaketon-Hall, 1983). Historians who have researched the activities of Special Operations Executive (SOE) dismiss these stories as nonsense but, knowing Churchill's love of intrigue, it might be wiser to keep an open mind.
14. ADM 199/829, Folio 52 (PRO, Kew).
15. Interview with Mr Copeland, Bermuda, November 1990.
16. *Who Killed Surcouf?, op. cit.*, 60.
17. The last of the L-Class was *L-11* which was scrapped on November 28 1923, while *L-9* was scrapped on May 4 that same year. No L-Class submarines were brought back for service during World War II. However, a number of other US Navy submarines were recommissioned, including nineteen O-Class and R-Class and sixteen S-Class, and nine of these were transferred to the Royal Navy in 1941–2. *R-17* was transferred on March 9 1942, renamed HMS *P-512*, and operated out of Bermuda as a Royal Canadian Navy training boat, finally being returned to America in 1945. Several other ex-US Navy submarines operated out of Bermuda so it would not have been unusual to find ex-American submarines there at the same time as *Surcouf*, but none would have been of the L-Class. (The author is indebted to Mr Kenneth C Henry, of Florida, for his expert assistance in tracing the history of these submarines.)
18. *Who Killed Surcouf?, op. cit.*, 61.
19. *Warship International*, Issue No. 2, 1980, letter from Paul Miller, of Milton, Wisconsin, USA, 191–2.
20. *Argosy Magazine*, New York, January 1967, vol 364, No. 1, 56.
21. The area around Long Island is regularly and extensively surveyed by the US Navy's Hydrographic Department, and it is difficult to believe that a wreck the size of *Surcouf* (which would give a particularly clear image on both sonar and magnetometer) could pass unnoticed, while the position of every German U-boat sunk during World War II is well known.
22. *Who Killed Surcouf?, op. cit.*, 66.
23. Serial TR 114-42, Record Group 80, Sec Nav/CNO, Secret File, L 11-1/EF30 (National Archives, Washington).
24. ADM 199/829 (PRO, Kew).
25. Vincennes Archives, Paris.
26. Kindly made available by Mr Gus Britton of the RN Submarine Museum.
27. Interview, Bermuda, November 1990.
28. Harcourt Brace, New York, 1976. The book was strongly criticized for numerous errors and distortions, the best account of which is to be found in Nigel West's *Unreliable Witness* (Weidenfeld & Nicolson, 1984).
29. Interviews with Walter Seymour and Donald Bernard, Bermuda, Novem-

ber 1990.

30. Interview with Mrs Joan McGillary, Florida, December 1990.

31. *Who Killed Surcouf?, op. cit.*, 54.

32. Letter from Emil P Moschella, FBI, Freedom of Information ref. no. 267,716, August 26 1986.

CHAPTER 10
THE FINAL HOURS

Having dealt with the mythology, we can now consider what facts are known concerning the last days of *Surcouf* prior to the collision between the *Thompson Lykes* and an unidentified vessel at 10.30 pm on the night of February 18 1942.

From the time *Surcouf* left Bermuda on February 12 she was never seen again. *Surcouf*'s sailing orders required her to make the 1610 nautical mile journey to Colon in 161 hours, leaving Bermuda at 3 pm on February 12 and arriving off Colon at 8 am on February 19, there being no change in time zones. Ignoring tidal flows and wind, this required an average speed of 10 knots which matched *Surcouf*'s normal cruising speed.

Assuming *Surcouf* maintained an average 10 knots throughout her voyage her positions would have been approximately:[1]

3 pm February 12	leaves Bermuda
3 pm February 13	28°56'N 67°25'W
3 pm February 14	25°40'N 69°50'W
3 pm February 15	22°25'N 72°20'W
3 pm February 16	19°05'N 74°20'W
3 pm February 17	15°40'N 76°35'W
3 pm February 18	12°05'N 78°24'W
10.30 pm	11°10'N 79°05'W

For the first three days *Surcouf* maintained a course of 215°

south-west from Bermuda across the ocean where there was little chance of her being sighted. But, at about 3 pm on February 15, *Surcouf* started her passage through the narrow Caicos Passage, and then, passing to the west of Great Inagua Island, early on the morning of February 16 entered the forty-mile wide Windward Passage, between the US Navy's base at Guantanamo, in Cuba, and Haiti. *Surcouf* passed within five miles of Navassa Island that night and, at around 7 am the following morning (February 17) was off the Morant Cays, a small group of islands forty-five miles south-west of Kingston, Jamaica, where the Royal Navy was on extra alert for German *U-boats* that had been active in the area, and had also been given the details of *Surcouf*'s voyage.

What makes the lack of any sighting stranger than usual is that, because of her defective electric motor, *Surcouf* had to make the entire journey on the surface, whereas normally a submarine would travel submerged during the day, and then continue on the surface only at night while recharging her batteries. One might therefore have expected the largest submarine in the world to have been noticed at some time during the period late on February 15 to early morning on the 17th when she was close to land from which air patrols were regularly being sent out to look for German *U-boats*, and in the middle of a busy shipping area. Only poor visibility could have hampered a sighting.

Taking the sinister viewpoint, one could argue that there is, therefore, no evidence that after leaving Bermuda, *Surcouf* followed her orders and went south at all. But equally there is no confirmed report of her being sighted anywhere else after February 12. Is it possible that Blaison changed his route? If Blaison had discovered the limpet mines on his vessel after leaving Bermuda, he would have had every reason for altering course and making for Vichy-held Martinique, thus accounting for Hoover's letter to Admiral Wilkinson.

On the other hand, if the limpet mines were never placed, then Blaison would have been unlikely to vary his route because, the day before *Surcouf* sailed, the US Navy issued the following message to all its Atlantic and Caribbean stations including Panama:

> Allied submarine notice. Free French submarine *Surcouf*
> leaves Bermuda 1800 Zed [Z being Greenwich Mean
> Time five hours ahead of local Caribbean time] 12
> February via Caicos and Windward passages due Colon
> 1300 Z 19 February. Total bombing restrictions 15 miles
> each side of tract and 120 miles ahead and astern.[2]

This is known as a 'submarine moving haven'[3] and, for British
submarines, it would be twenty to thirty miles ahead and
seventy to eighty miles astern, based on the assumption that a
submarine was more likely to be behind, rather than ahead of
her schedule. The moving haven for *Surcouf* was very much
larger presumably because of her poor record of seamanship
and reliability. Had Blaison varied his course from that given to
the Americans he would have been inviting attack from a jittery
US Army Air Corps in the early days of the war.

Surcouf's position at 3 pm on February 18 was 110 miles from
the collision point so, assuming she maintained 10 knots for the
next seven and a half hours, she would still be about thirty-five
miles, or three and a half hours away at 10.30 pm. This is a very
insignificant distance at the end of a six-day voyage, but indicates that *Surcouf* was unlikely to have been ahead of her
schedule, even assuming she had maintained her best average
speed of 10 knots for the entire period and never varied from the
most direct route.

Did *Surcouf* maintain an average speed of 10 knots for those
six days? On the experience of her previous four voyages it
would be remarkable if *Surcouf* managed to run for six days
without having some technical problems, especially as she was
relying on only one engine. Normally she made a routine dive
each day, usually at 6 am, to test out all the systems but, knowing her tendency to go out of control even when both electric
motors were working, it is unlikely this procedure was adhered
to during this voyage. However, if she had cause to dive for any
other reason, such as sighting a suspicious surface vessel or air-

186

craft, then that would have delayed her.

If *Surcouf* had only averaged 9 knots for the previous six days then, by 3 pm on February 18, she would be at approximately 14°05′N 77°24′W, or 235 miles from the collision point. Assuming she covered seventy miles in the next seven and a half hours that would place her 167 miles, or nearly eighteen hours, away making it impossible for her to have been involved.

On February 22, the Admiralty told the US Navy that at 6 pm London time (or 1 pm local Caribbean time) on February 18, *Surcouf* had reached the position of 14°00′N 79°00′W, and was on a course of 210° at 10 knots.[4] This meant that in the 142 hours since *Surcouf* left Bermuda she had covered only 1326 nautical miles, giving an average speed of only 9 knots, although the Admiralty was claiming she was now on course at 10 knots. It also meant that *Surcouf* had 284 nautical miles to go before reaching Colon and, as that would take over twenty-eight hours, plainly *Surcouf* was well behind schedule and would not reach Colon until at least 6 pm on February 19, some ten hours late.

But the Admiralty's coordinates also placed *Surcouf* 204 nautical miles from the collision point at 10°40′N 79°31′W. It would take *Surcouf* twenty hours to cover that distance, yet the *Thompson Lykes* hit another vessel only nine and a half ½ hours later at 10.30 pm that same day. In other words *Surcouf* would still be over 100 miles away. Furthermore, the Admiralty's position showed *Surcouf* eighty-five miles to the west of the direct track from Navassa Island to Colon.

How did the Admiralty know this since *Surcouf* would certainly not have broken radio silence to report her position? According to the distinguished British submariner, Rear Admiral Sir David Scott, the report is worthless as its impreciseness with all the zeroes shows it must have been an estimate, probably made by a young inexperienced officer 'who had a couple of gins too many before lunch'.

If this were so, then it raises two further points. First, why choose 1 pm on February 18 when it would have been more logical to use the impact time of 10.30 pm? There was nothing special about 1 pm. Second, if the Admiralty had not received any sighting of *Surcouf* during the previous six days, why not tell the Americans this, adding that they could only assume that, if *Surcouf* had maintained a speed of 10 knots, she would have been in the collision area at 10.30 pm?

But the US Navy could have worked that out themselves, since they already had a copy of *Surcouf*'s sailing orders. In this case the Americans would have mentioned that the Admiralty's 1 pm position was only a guess.

When evaluating any historical anomaly, it is always wise to allow for cock-up rather than conspiracy but, even so, it is strange that an inexperienced officer was allowed to send the US Navy a report about the loss of this highly controversial submarine without first checking it with a more experienced peson.

What makes all this even more bizarre is that not only did the US Navy accept the Admiralty's position for *Surcouf* as accurate, and evidently did not check it on a chart, he then confused matters even further by saying:

> If *Surcouf* had been about 55 miles behind the
> Admiralty's reported position at 6 pm [London time, 1
> pm local time], 18 February, the *Surcouf* would have
> been in the area where the merchant ship reported her
> ramming and sinking a craft believed to have been a
> submarine.

Plainly this is absurd for that would have place *Surcouf* over 150 miles from the collision point. Perhaps Low was yet another inexperienced officer but, even if we generously assume that he meant 'ahead' and not 'behind' (although no one else ever has) that would still put *Surcouf* fifty miles, or five hours, away from the *Thompson Lykes* at 10.30 pm on February 18. Low's memorandum of February 23 then went to Captain Schuirman USN, who saw nothing amiss, and was subsequently quoted in at least a dozen other reports over the next year.

However when Admiral Auboynau, of the Free French navy in London, saw the Navy's report, he wrote in the margin: 'Should not the Admiralty position read 11°00′N 79°00′W?'[5] In a later report he stated:

> (6) If the location and the time of the ramming [as
> indicated by the *Thompson Lykes*] are taken into
> account, and not the Admiralty 1 pm position, *Surcouf*
> was a few hours in advance on its normal course to reach
> the Panama Canal.

Auboynau's argument is remarkably unconvincing for two
reasons. First, all he has done is to move *Surcouf*'s position at 1
pm on February 18 forward by 180 miles by altering the northerly coordinate from 14° to 11°, and then claiming that she must
have been in advance of her schedule. But there is no more evidence to support that conclusion than the Admiralty's position.
If one assumes *Surcouf* used the most direct route from Navassa
Island to Colon, and maintained 10 knots, she was two to three
hours behind her schedule.

Second, if Auboynau believed the Admiralty were wrong,
why did he not immediately ask how their 1 pm position had
been calculated and if it was based on a sighting? It has been
argued that the Admiralty was very busy with other more important matters in the middle of a war, but it would have been
easy to check on what the position was based as it takes less than
five minutes to plot *Surcouf*'s track from Bermuda to Colon on
the relevant chart.

But despite their suspicions that they were not being told the
truth, neither Auboynau nor anyone else at the Free French
naval headquarters ever went back to the Admiralty to check
the facts, nor has it ever been mentioned in all the many stories
about *Surcouf* these past forty years.

Turning now to the *Thompson Lykes*, the inquiry clearly
showed that there was nothing unusual about the details of her
voyage which was the return leg of her normal round trip from
New Orleans to the Panama Canal via Cuba.[6] Since Johnson
was authorized to take the route of his choice to Cuba, and had
evidently not been told anything about *Surcouf*, he could hardly
have deliberately sought her out to ram. Even if Johnson had

189

been given *Surcouf's* sailing orders it is hard to see what he could have done unless, of course the US Navy permitted him to show some navigation lights. Neither ship had radar and *Surcouf's* orders were not precise enough to enable him to estimate her likely position at the end of a 1600-mile voyage.

A good deal of the inquiry was taken up discussing whether the lookouts on board the *Thompson Lykes* could have seen the other vessel earlier. Obviously if there had been a lookout position right up in the bow he would have been 150 feet nearer, but as there was no telephone at the bow having someone there would have been of no value. Normally the lookout in the crow's-nest has the best view except, as in this case, of a vessel lying very low, or even partly submerged, in the water.

Dealing with the question of the white light that first warned the *Thompson Lykes* of the presence of another vessel, it is worth noting that Burney had mentioned in his reports that:

> On the way from Halifax to Bermuda, as indeed at all times, the officer of the watch [on the bridge] would use the small hand-flashing lamp, quite unshaded, in order to see the bearing indicators.[7]

As to the identity of the other vessel, although the inquiry did its best to establish this, it was unable to produce any definite evidence mainly because those with the best view had the least sea-going experience. Although the descriptions speak of a long, cigar-shaped vessel, when the *Thompson Lykes* first got back to Cristobal it was thought she might have hit a small armed launch. Exactly what such a launch would have been doing in the middle of the Caribbean at night no one has ever tried to explain and, if one had been lost, then its failure to return to port would surely have been noticed.

Another theory that has been advanced is that the vessel was one of the many small oil tankers that plied these waters thus accounting for the crude oil on the surface after the collision. Apart from the basic problem of why such a tanker's loss would not have been reported, evidence about the oil is conflicting and, since no one bothered to take samples, it could have been bunker fuel or diesel oil.[8]

Probably the mot contentious issue was that of the men briefly seen in the water and their shouts for help. Myers' description of a man in a 'white sweat shirt with white sleeves' could have referred to a white sweater of the type normally worn by British submariners or it might have been the white top worn by most sailors. The question of the shouts for help in English is complicated by the fact that few of *Surcouf*'s crew spoke English. Everyone who met the crew of *Surcouf* commented on the difficulty they had making themselves understood because the crew spoke in such a strong local *patois* and knew no English.

In an emergency, one would expect a Frenchman to use the expression *'m'aidez'*[9] rather than 'help' although, of course, a member of the liaison team might have been on the bridge, wearing a British Navy issue white sweater and shouting in English.

That the *Thompson Lykes* hit something is not in doubt, but the damage was certainly not as extensive as one might expect from a collision between a 6700-ton steamer and a 4000-ton submarine. To get a totally objective opinion of what might have caused the damage to the *Thompson Lykes*, the two photographs of her damaged hull were examined by Dennis Pascoe, chairman of the Falmouth Ship Repair Yard in Cornwall, who has a long experience of repairing vessels damaged by collision. Without being given any details of the circumstances he commented:

I agree that the photographs indicate that the other unidentified vessel would appear to have passed from right to left of *Thompson Lykes*, to have rubbed down the port side and with the light draft forward and trim by the stern was partly ridden over at least.

The indent of the 12' 0" mark on the bow of the *Thompson Lykes* would indicate a vessel with a small freeboard above the sea only some 2' 0" approximately. Usually the collision of steel vessels causes more ragged

191

damaged with steel plating cut and holed . . . [and] . . . through part submersion [could] have pushed *Thompson Lykes*' bow over as the photographs indicate . . . a submarine with small freeboard would not be beyond consideration . . . the rounded hull of a submarine would tend to cause less cutting and penetration of the other vessel.

Submarines were fitted with a horizontal casing top and it could have been the corner of that structure which caused the indent at the 12' 0" draft; there would of course be nothing above that casing if the impact point came aft of the conning tower.[10]

This opinion fits well with all the evidence that the enquiry produced which showed that the other vessel was very low in the water and accorded with the profile of a submarine 'trimmed down', that is to say, as low as possible in the water. We know that the light was first seen to the right (starboard) and then ahead, the collision occurring shortly afterwards which means that the point of impact would have been aft of the conning tower.

Several witnesses thought the freighter had lifted up out of the water or 'slid on a beach', thus suggesting the bow of the *Thompson Lykes* rode up over the aft portion of *Surcouf* as Dennis Pascoe mentioned. The force of the collision at the rear of *Surcouf* would have forced it round so that it slid down the left (port) side of the *Thompson Lykes* before disappearing into the darkness.

Since the only submarine known to be in the area was *Surcouf* (no German *U-boats* were lost around this time in the Caribbean from any cause[11]), it is sensible to accept that the other vessel must have been *Surcouf* notwithstanding all the conflicting evidence about her position and, of course, whether she was destroyed by limpet mines shortly after leaving Bermuda.

The question that remains is, therefore, was the impact sufficiently serious to sink *Surcouf* immediately? The damage to the *Thompson Lykes* indicates the freighter had not cut into the central section of the hull of the other vessel, and it is therefore likely that *Surcouf* did not sink but drifted on, perhaps still under its own power, in a semi-waterlogged state. Because the *Thompson Lykes* did not reverse engines immediately, it travelled on a considerable distance before turning round and coming back to the approximate position of the impact. Likewise, *Surcouf* would have continued on in the opposite direction.

The *Thompson Lykes* remained in the area of the collision until the next morning and, even when joined by the USS *Tatnall* and *Barry*, no attempt was made to widen the search area nor were any aircraft called in to help until later. It was merely assumed that the other vessel had sunk in the immediate area although there was no evidence or wreckage to prove this one way or the other.

Some weeks after *Surcouf* vanished, Charles Q Peters, a salvage diver with the US Navy Construction Battalion (usually known as the 'Seabees') at the Coco Solo navy base at the Atlantic entrance to the Panama Canal, heard reports that *Surcouf* had been bombed by the US Army Air Corps (USAAC) near the Panama coast at San Blas, although Peters was unclear whether the bombing had been deliberate or accidental. After the war, when he had left the US Navy, Peters was in charge of the Pan American Airways radio beacon, situated on top of a small hill on San Blas Point, and he heard the story again from some of the local Cuna Indians that, after the bombing, *Surcouf* had drifted towards the coast and finally sunk off the island of Chi Chi Mey in the Archipelago de las Mulatas.

A similar story was also heard by José Garcia,[12] a member of an old-established Spanish merchant family, who operated small trading boats along the Atlantic coast of Panama mainly engaged in the coconut and copra trade which, at that time, was centred around the San Blas area. In February 1942, Garcia had helped local Indians to bury the bodies of some sailors that had been washed up on the coast in the *Guaca*, or foreigners', Cemetery on San Blas point.

These stories would probably have remained untold had it not been for the arrival of John Mann in the area. A quite remarkable and charming character, Mann was born in 1928 in Ohio and later served in the US Marine Corps, after which he became a highly skilled welder at the Lincoln Electric Company in Cleveland. During a recession in the early 1950s Mann was laid off and, deciding he would like to learn Spanish, bought a donkey for $3 and proceeded to walk to Mexico.

Having learned Spanish, Mann explored further with his donkey, and eventually ended up in Panama at San Blas and decided to stay. Mann sold the donkey, moved on to one of the tiny islands in the area, built himself a house, and then taught himself how to construct a boat. For the next twenty-seven years Mann lived amongst the gentle Cuna Indians and today is not only their friend, but is regarded as one of the foremost authorities on their lifestyle and, although no longer living on his idyllic island, takes small parties of tourists to visit San Blas and other remote areas of Panama.

Mann met Peters (then running the airways beacon) and Garcia when he first arrived at San Blas and in due course heard the story about the *Surcouf* having been bombed and lying off the coast but, because he knew nothing else about the vessel, did not consider the tale particularly important as German *U-boats* had also been sunk in the area during the war.

The USAAC unit stationed in Panama in 1942 was the 6th Bombardment Group (Heavy) of the 6th Air Force.[13] It had begun life in September 1919 at France Field airbase as the 3rd Observation Group for the Panama Canal Zone, equipped with R-4 and DH-4 aircraft. After changing its name several times, by 1942 it was using A-17 and B-17 aircraft and was also operating out of Rio Hato air base where the 3rd Bombardment Squadron was located under the command of Colonel Henry K Mooney.

The Rio Hato air base (then no more than a grass landing strip) had been hastily brought into service on December 9 1941 following the Japanese attack on Pearl Harbor and, amongst its personnel, was an eager twenty-three-year-old Lieutenant Harold A Staley.[14] Staley was born in January 1919 at Genesco,

194

New York, and graduated from Genesco High School and Mechanics Institute, thereafter going to work for the Eastman Kodak Company at Rochester. In March 1941, Staley joined the USAAC and completed his flying training at Montgomery Field, Alabama, on October 30. He was first posted to France Field, and then on the outbreak of war to Rio Hato.

Staley's first task was to report to his commanding officer, Colonel Mooney, a pre-war regular Air Corps officer of great skill and also a martinet when it came to discipline. Years later Mooney met up with Staley again who reminded him on that first visit that one of his shirt buttons was broken. Staley then had to learn to use a 0.45-calibre pistol so he could protect himself and the air base but, when he achieved this, the sergeant said he had no ammunition to spare and 'If the Japs land, throw it at them'. Staley's A-17 was a single-engined attack (A) aircraft, with a cruising speed of about 130 mph, which carried four 100-pound bombs and had two .30-calibre machine guns firing forward.

At 7.13 am on February 19 1942 (the morning after the collision) Bomber Command headquarters in Panama sent a message to Staley's squadron at Rio Hato ordering them to attack a submarine at position R-13. The use of the coordinate R-13 is a mystery because on all other occasions the attack position was given either in longitude and latitude or, as on February 16, to attack a submarine '4 miles off Chagress River'.

Because a coordinate like R-13 had never been used before its location remained a mystery until the author interviewed Colonel Art Irwin in California, who had served in Panama from mid 1943.[15] He explained that R-13 was taken from the world time-zone chart used by the American services (see page 202) and R was the sector that ran south from America, down across Cuba to Panama. Colonel Irwin explained that there were a series of vertical north–south sectors running down from Cuba to Panama, and that the 13th was some fifty to sixty miles off the Atlantic coast of Panama. Unfortunately neither Colonel Irwin, nor any of the relevant archival material, was able to explain why this reference system had not been used on other

195

occasions.

Colonel Mooney ordered two A-17s and one B-18 (a twin-engined bomber that carried three 300-pound bombs), to be despatched.[16] Unfortunately, one of the A-17s, piloted by Lieutenant Pryor, broke its tailwheel during takeoff, and Staley was ordered to replace him, taking off at 8 am. Staley found the submarine, 'a very large one', low in the water as if about to submerge, dropped four bombs and believed he had hit it, and then circled the area for ten minutes and saw it disappear, finally getting back to Rio Hato at 9.35 am. It's tailwheel repaired, Lieutenant Pryor's A17 also dropped its bombs on the submarine, but the B-18 bomber, piloted by Lieutenant Terry reported on his return to Lieutenant Wood that he had been unable to find the target. Thus in total eight 100-pound bombs were dropped on the submarine.

Both Staley and Pryor told Wood they had bombed the submarine and, it seems, assumed it was either Japanese or German. Although they had been briefed before the attack no mention was made about an allied submarine being in the area. The bombing restrictions imposed for *Surcouf*'s voyage to Panama were not due to end until 8 am, but perhaps in the excitement these instructions were overlooked.

At 11.47 am, Wood sent a teletype message to headquarters in Panama about the mission but nothing happened until, at 1.10 am the following morning (February 20) a secret message in an 'officer only' code (that had to be decoded by Lieutenants Bronson and Tarkenton) was received from Bomber Command. This was most unusual and nowhere else in the squadron's daily log during all its years in Panama is there mention of a similar secret message being received following a mission. Was this message connected with the attack on the submarine, and does it refer to the fact that a large French submarine was believed to have been in collision in the area, and that the 'enemy submarine' might have been *Surcouf*? Unfortunately, none of the messages passing between Rio Hato and Panama can now be found, while nothing was said at the time to any of the officers involved; for them it was just another day.

196

Certainly no Japanese submarine that might have looked like *Surcouf* was in the area, and there is no record of a German *U-boat* being sunk at that time. Therefore there is some reasonable evidence that it could have been *Surcouf*. But the evidence is far from complete and many obvious anomalies exist. For example, if *Surcouf* did not sink after the collision, why did Blaison not break radio silence and send a distress call to Colon? Had the impact caused flooding that destroyed all electrical power, or, having discovered the limpet mines had Blaison decided not to trust the allies? But, in that case, why was *Surcouf* still on course for Panama instead of faraway to the east near Martinique?

If one accepts that *Surcouf* did collide with the *Thompson Lykes* (and all the evidence certainly points that way) then it follows that the submarine had carried out its voyage from Bermuda to Panama in accordance with the Admiralty's instructions which, in turn, makes the limpet mine story – and their discovery – unlikely, as it does that *Surcouf* attempted to defect to Martinique.

On the other hand, if *Surcouf* did not collide with the freighter then, aside from having to produce an alternative vessel whose loss was never reported, it opens up a host of other possibilities, including the discovery of the limpet mines with all its ramifications.

If *Surcouf* did end its troubled life off San Blas, then it could not have found a more beautiful place to lie at rest for this is certainly Panama's Shangri-la. With John Mann as my guide, and Krish Persaud my pilot, Persaud's small aircraft climbed steadily away from Panama over the dense mist-shrouded Darien jungle until, as the storm clouds parted, we suddenly glimpsed the Atlantic coast and the great sweep of the bay that forms San Blas and its 400 islands; from a distance it looks like a great armada getting ready to sail.

As Krish brought the aircraft down lower, I could see some of the forty-eight little settlements, in which the 40,000 or so Cunas live, clustered on some of the islands. In the surrounding jungle, there are a few traces of the primitive farming that the Cunas

197

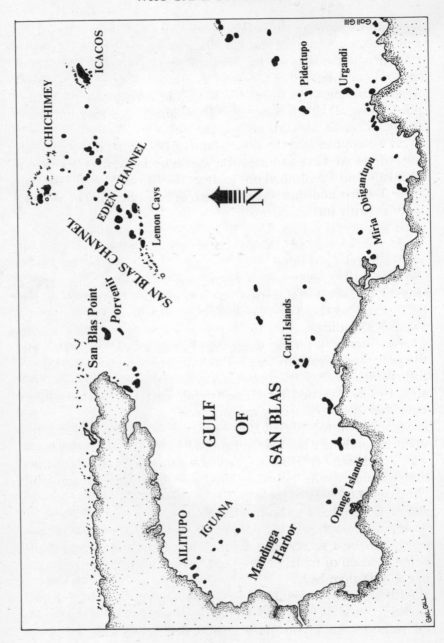

ICACOS

CHICHIMEY

Pidertupo

Urgandi

EDEN CHANNEL

Lemon Cays

Miria Obigantupu

SAN BLAS CHANNEL

San Blas Point

Porvenir

N

Carti Islands

GULF

OF

SAN BLAS

AILITUPO

IGUANA

Mandinga Harbor

Orange Islands

GAIL GILL

carry out each day providing them with the basic necessities. Fifty years ago during the war there was a significant military presence in San Blas with a radar station on San Blas Point, generators, and barracks for over a hundred men. In addition several landing strips were built to enable aircraft to ferry in supplies. Now all this has gone and the jungle has reclaimed virtually all traces of wartime occupation.

As we approached the little island of Pouvenir, its short landing strip looked even shorter, but Krish bounced his Cessna to a standstill and we climbed out to meet the Cuna people. The men wore T-shirts and shorts, the women dressed in tribal *moals* and sarongs with intricately woven motifs, while beads decorated their wrists and ankles. Unmarried women wear their hair long, while the married cut theirs urchin-style with the nose pierced with a heavy gold ring.

Independent, even haughty, and supremely confident of their way of life, we were ferried out in dug-out canoes across the 84°F water to the San Blas mainland with its thick mangrove swamps. Wading ashore through the mud, I was taken to the *Guaca* Cemetery on the side of a hill overlooking the bay. As the graves were roughly dug and the bodies not buried in coffins, little remains today apart from occasional depressions in the soft soil. But Garcia and his Cuna friends certainly buried sailors here shortly after *Surcouf* disappeared.

Standing on top of San Blas hill and looking out towards the open sea and the island of Chi Chi Mey, I suddenly felt my quest was complete. If *Surcouf* was the submarine accidentally bombed that day in February fifty years ago, then she must be lying out there where the water is less than 2000 feet deep, and should not be hard to find. After all her trials and tribulations, disappointments, and the personal agonies of her crew as they tried their best to serve in a cause few fully understood while being accused of treachery and cowardice, what better place for her to rest than here.

Although *Surcouf* and her crew may never have accomplished anything, at least I have been able to set to rest for ever some of the rumours and myths that so bedevilled her short career. *Sur-*

couf already has her official memorial, but the tranquillity and beauty of San Blas and its gentle people is surely a more poignant one to a grand design and its brave and gallant crew. Like many before them and since, they risked their lives serving their country, far from a home none would ever see again, knowing full well the perils of the sea. Now they lie at peace secure within its protection for all time.

NOTES

1. The author is most grateful to Lieutenant Commander John Pugh RN, Wrecks Officer, Ministry of Defence, Hydrographic Department, Taunton, for his expert advice and information concerning *Surcouf*'s last voyage.
2. Vincennes Archives, Paris.
3. Information kindly supplied by Admiral Sir David Scott, October 1990.
4. Memorandum from Captain FS Low, HQ Navy Department, Washington, DC, dated February 23 1942, to Captain Schuirman (Vincennes Archives, Paris, and Naval Historical Center, Washington Navy Yard).
5. These handwritten comments only appear on the copy in the Vincennes Archives, Paris.
6. Which she always made alone and unescorted. How the story began that the *Thompson Lykes* was part of a convoy is unknown but is, perhaps, just another example of the confusion that surrounds *Surcouf*.
7. ADM 199/829 (PRO, Kew).
8. Nor did anyone think of taking samples of the paint marks on the damaged portion of the *Thompson Lykes*' hull which could have been analysed to see if it was similar to the paint used at the navy yard at Portsmouth where *Surcouf* was last repainted. When the British submarine *M-1* was lost following a collision with the Swedish steamer *Vidar*, in the English Channel on November 12 1925, samples of paint later found on the hull of the *Vidar* were found to be similar to the Admiralty grey paint used on *M-1*, (ADM 116/2292 & 2293, PRO, Kew).
9. An expression for an emergency that is today universally used as 'Mayday'.
10. Letter to author July 24 1987. It is worth remembering that the *Thompson Lykes* was trimmed so that the bow was riding higher than normal.
11. The RN Submarine Museum holds detailed records of exactly when, where, and how every *U-boat* was lost during World War II.
12. Both Charles Peters and José Garcia are dead, and the author is grateful to John Mann and Edward James for information based on various conversations with them over the years.

13. *Air Force Combat Units of World War II*, edited by M Maurer (Office of Air Force History, Washington, DC, 1983), *History of the Caribbean Air Force, 8 May 1941 – 6 March 1942* (Archives of the AAF Historical Office), original date unknown, but declassified February 29 1960, all kindly supplied by the Research Division, HQ USAF Historical Research Center, Maxwell AFB, Alabama.

14. Interview, Rochester, New York, December 1990. After leaving Panama, Colonel Staley served with great distinction in the Pacific theatre of operations flying more than sixty-eight missions against the Japanese in his Boeing B-17 Flying Fortress named 'Black Jack'. After returning to America in 1943, 'Black Jack' was hit by enemy fire off New Guinea and the crew had to ditch but were all saved. In 1987 the remarkably well-preserved wreck of 'Black Jack' was found by Australian divers on the sea bed. Colonel Staley returned to the South Pacific in late 1943 and flew a further thirty-one missions against the Japanese in B-24 Liberator bombers before the surrender in 1945.

15. Interview, Navato, California, 1990.

16. Log book of the 3rd Bombardment Squadron kindly made available by the USAF Historical Center, Maxwell AFB, Alabama.

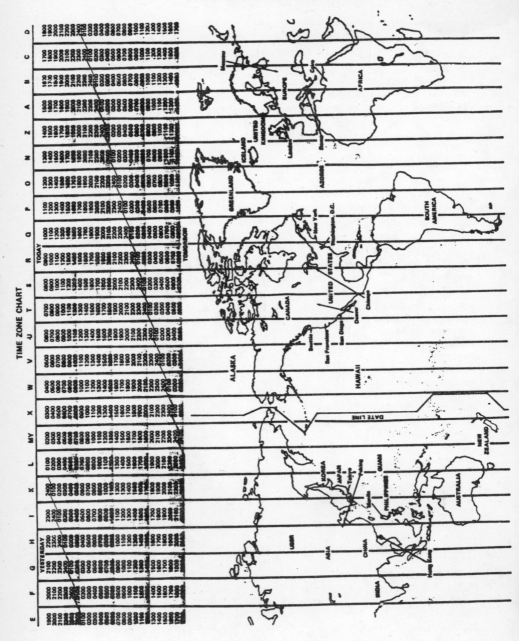

INDEX

203